absent friend
a seduction of innocent minds

COLLECTED POEMS OF

Abbey Laurel-Smith
(Abiodun Oladewa)

WRITER'S AWARD IN POETRY,
2004, VSC, JOHNSON. VERMONT

DOROTHY BULEY FELLOWSHIP FOR PASTEL
ARTIST, 2002 VSC, JOHNSON. VERMONT

SOUTH FLORIDA'S ARTIST OF THE MONTH,
NOVEMBER, 2002

© 2004 by ABBEY LAUREL-SMITH (ABIODUN OLADEWA).
All rights reserved.

No part of this book may be reproduced, stored in a retrieval system, or transmitted by any means, electronic, mechanical, photocopying, recording, or otherwise, without written permission from the author.

First published by AuthorHouse 05/03/04

ISBN: 1-4184-6280-2 (e-book)
ISBN: 1-4184-4483-9 (Paperback)

Library of Congress Control Number: 2003195181

This book is printed on acid free paper.

Printed in the United States of America
Bloomington, IN

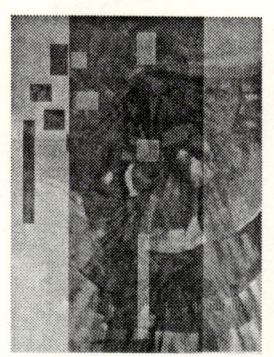

drawings and paintings ©1989 – 1993, 2000 – 2003
by ABIODUN OLADEWA (ABBEY LAUREL-SMITH)
All rights reserved.

About the Author

**ABBEY LAUREL-SMITH
(ABIODUN OLADEWA)**

Abbey Laurel-Smith (Abiodun Oladewa) was born on December 27, 1965, at Igboora, in the Western part of Nigeria, West Africa. He studied Fine Art at The Polytechnic of Ibadan, Nigeria. He also studied History of Art and Heritage Management in England and Venice, courtesy of The University of Buckingham, its prestigious Waddesdon Manor and Oxford Brookes University, all in neighborly Buckinghamshire and Oxfordshire.

Now a Maine resident, he has lived in the states of New Jersey (Matawan) Florida (Miami Beach) since the year 2000 and has just been given a writers' award in Poetry, by the Vermont Studio Center, Johnson, Vermont.

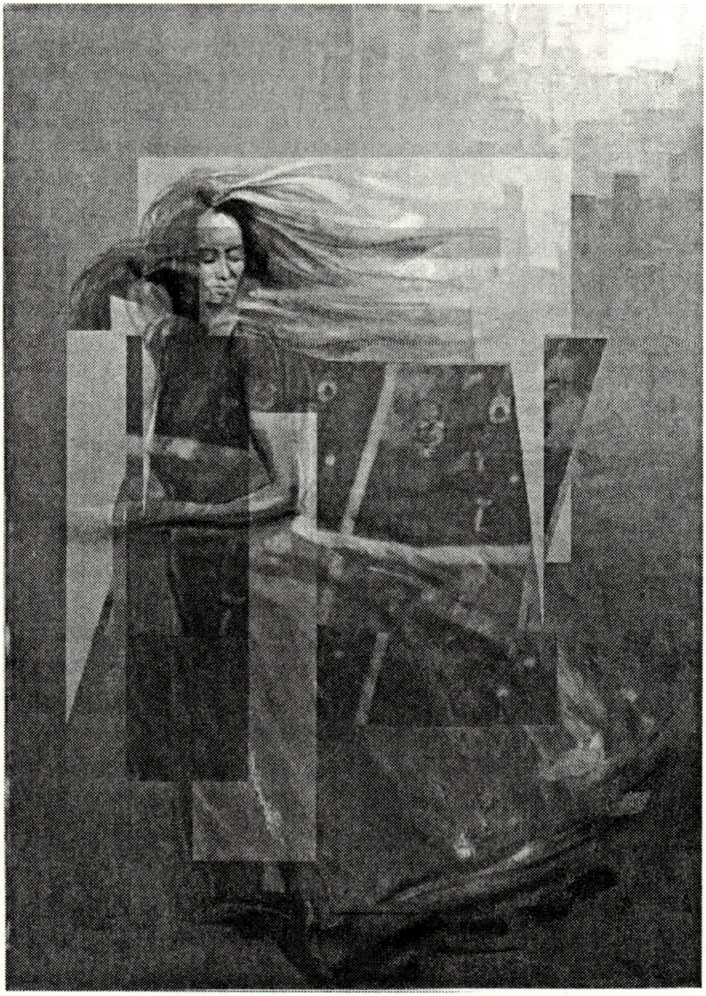

About the Author	iii
My Mother's Voice	1
I never even knew My own Soul…	7
Between Her face and Mine	10
Your breath on my brow	11
Loni	21
Let me be your absent friend	27
A powdered Rose	28
I remember thee my country, as my home…	32
Now	39
Timbuktu	51
Every Woman	55
My true breath, I held	60
The greatness of Death	81
I hope it doesn't rain tonight	98
Before myself	104
Nicole Peskin	113
Death of all Dreams	123
A Woebegone Song	132
Turning Tables	140
Dear Sgt Major	163
New York	170
The joy of Castle Rising	173
A bottled condemnation	176
Between hanging and mid life crises	177
To my Grandmother (the illiterate)	180
The garden of my youth	186
Certain things	198
Six feet under	202
La Citta del Sole	203
I paid a price under a tree	212
Patience is a Fool's gift	213

A concert in the wind 214

let me be your absent friend

My Mother's Voice

I could hear my Mother's voice
Charming my blood with wise words…

I never understood why
Her persuasive choice of words
And their Christian manner of articulation,
Were soothing yet, never intended to please.
But I will always remain Her Child
One that She fed many times,
And I will always remain Her only Son
One that She dearly loved.

The rest of my life, I will spend
Chewing on her words; especially those
That I will hereby share with you:
"There are those times in our lives,
When we fall victim to public lust
And like the Good Samaritan,
We become victims of our own adventure."

This is My own Mother's voice
Charming My soul with wise words,
As if they were not meant to please,
As if they were not meant to amuse,
Whilst they feed and grow on me.

But the God of adventure took me away,
Away from Her lap, away from Her reach
Yet in My process of an arty advancement,
I must admit to you Loni and others, that,

Her tongue still remains as sweet
As they were, when I came to being,
As they were, when I took my first breath,
And as soothing, as they would forever be,
From that unforgettable seventh day of my being;
When Adigun Onikola, omo asani l'ogbe gb'owo
Called in to provide the beauty of circumcision.

Somehow,
I will always remain Her Child
And one that She fed many times,
I will always remain Her only Son
And one that She dearly loved.

For as long as I breathe this air
That I can never ever see, then
I will always hear the tune
of My Mother's soothing voice
Charming and comforting Her only Son's soul,
As if those words were never meant to please
And as if those words were never intended to amuse,
Whilst they continue to feed and grow on me.

Funny as it may be,
I could never ever understand,
Why her persuasive choice of words
And their Christian manner of articulation,
Were so soothing but never intended to please.
Therefore, in Her eyes, I will always be
No Other than remain Her only Son
And One that She dearly loved.

I guess
I will forever hear My Mother's voice

let me be your absent friend

Charming my blood with wise words.
I will forever hear her lovely voice
Stained by the sweet taste of Ibadan,
As it pours forth from her tongue.
And in My mind, and I will always be
No Other than Her only Son,
One that She dearly loved.

Charm

The charm of your open arms,
I've grown to know.
The nature of your smile,
I could trace without a line.
For the curves of your cheek bones,
Are no longer strange
To my soft childly kisses.

Your tears,
I do not wish to see,
For yours is a fabric, that gives life…

If all hearts should be mellow

In your arms, all hearts will be mellow
And I shall never be found wanting
For in the midst of a friendly company
I shall be,
And the voices of many a thousand minds
Shall drown the orchestra of sorrows
Of tales and of other woes
That keeps creeping up into your lovely ears,
For sad songs are not meant to be yours…

By my Tongue's worth

By my tongue's worth, I confess my heart,
For I might have exposed myself
Before the judgment of your thoughts.
Think I might have pressed on too far
Before the journey even starts.
But being stirred by a deep devotion
When through a Cleopatra I passed,
Is a labor blessed by providence
For through my tongue's worth
I hereby confess my heart
That ye shall lead and embrace me
And lift this love that I bear
With that that lives in thee, with care,
Like a little child heaved on both hands.

So blessed in difficulty was I, that
I never even knew My own Soul...

You made me feel, as if,
I never knew my own soul.
You made me feel, as if,
My own soul never existed.
When in actual fact
It existed in structural sections
And flourishes between boundaries
Of hate, of love
Of sorrows and of woes,
Like most 20th century states.

You may be right, that,
I never knew my own soul.
And you may be right, that,
My soul is no longer mine.
When in actual fact
These boundaries of change and migration
Have toughened the symbolic system
Of my soul, my tradition
And also of my religion - affected,
Like most 20th century states.

My conviction now resides
In what you called structural sections,
And my symbolic system thus changed,
But my belief remains like that of Moses;
Hard and blessed in difficulty.
It has never been so rich for it to die
Without its sweet pain pouring forth.
And it has never been made for it to die

Unloved and unrecognized abroad.

I therefore fix every quarter of my love
On that body that I thee worshipped
For its fullness and beauteous presence
Means everything we see is bumptiously blessed.

A Modiglianesque Heritage

A tussle with her beautiful mind
I've always found to be fascinating.
And a tussle of a visual type
I always prolonged for their aesthetics,
But a tussle with a Cleopatra's breath,
Trickling down the back of my neck
I've never been privileged to share.

So, tell me in your Modiglianesque heritage,
What is it like, exchanging smiles at dawn?
What is it like, waking up in your arms?

Your toes I might never ever see, before sunrise,
And the qualities of your hidden footsteps,
The world might never ever see, for once.
As She walked out of Her painted state
Where no frame, no wall, nor a canvas
Could ever hold Her in place.

She's the one – the only one out of many
Who brought dead pigments back to life
By breathing their textures into our senses,
And thus activating a feeling for seeing.

Now, She's no longer a walled treasure
Where she used to be the Other's treasure
Regaled in a permanently varnished state,
For the benefit of a few lucky bastards

And their ever prying eyes – to roam, and to explore.

Between Her face and Mine

Only a few inches of the ruler
Stands between her face and mine
For we are both aware
Of what might happen, - if they touch.
I am not against kisses and
Neither was she suffering
From a fatigue of a kind.

We fed and shouldered nature,
With a lover's light,
With sited body postures -
Hers inclined to mine.

In the dark depth of her eyes
Was I, lustfully consumed, whilst
Both circular spots beneath her brow
Consumed the varnish off my soul.

Her ideal nose could have made
The best of Caesar's army – blush
And the perfect poise of her luscious lips
Would make the bones of a Caesar

And a Mark Anthony blush in their graves,
Their Roman souls will be reawakened
And Cleopatra will be forgotten
For Cleopatra's nose was never as perfect…

let me be your absent friend

Your breath on my brow

Though heavy on my brow,
And blowing away my reality,
Your breath; if I may say,
Is always gentle on my memory.
Its sweetness, I consumed
And its lightness, I still recall.

I wonder how your warm grip
Never strangled my breath,
And how I never did cringe
Nor keep away from the splendor
That your fingertips bring;
Into every plucked path
That you led me through.

So happy is your name,
That I from now must confess
That the memory of your breath
Kept my brow alive and straight.

Lead me along like a Child
That's never learned to walk,
Teach me again to speak
In a language that only you
And no one else could decipher.

Then and maybe I shall
No longer spend my days,
Watching the dance of the Tombs
At sunset. Maybe I shall
No longer weep over bungled prices;

Those prices of a lifetime
Being consumed by a muddy soil
(One that we used to tread on
And one that now consumes
The best gifts of a lifetime).

For we shall be too busy
Learning to smile again.

let me be your absent friend

In the light of the true cross
"Can I see another's woe, and not be in sorrow too"
William Blake 1757 - 1827

Jesus had many Lovers during his lifetime
And he still does have many today,
Yet only one was willing to share his burden.
A Simon of Libya shared part of his last passions
(The burden of carrying a true cross like a poor
Atlas carrying the world on his shoulders).

Therefore,
In the light of the true cross, I read your love, and
In the light of the true cross, I'll favor a close reading.
For true love has many eyes, that influences the senses.
In lenient terms shall I state that: true love
Have many tributaries. And the sense could do no other
Than to interpret without an end in sight.

The politics of my poem
Would be focused on that of a true love
Of which the dictum of my readership
Will be like the wood of the true cross.
It will be bundled across frontiers of gender
And the grains and the grooves of my Cleopatra
Will thus be disguised as my poetic bride
Of whom piety shall never be scared to silence,

But what shall I do about
The moments of the previously past?
How do I relate to the past?
And those times gone by

Or even those beyond me?
If I tread through like a finite state,
The notion of what is adequately right
Becomes hazy and unclear and so will be
- My pen and my state of mind.

My knees are as weak as my heart,
And at this stage, I am no longer
Sure of my most appropriate stance
For neither have I been as consoling
As others do when they love to ignore.
I fear the sense of an ending
And I am not as thrilled to discover
That I can do no other
Than to civilize or to humanize
Those moments condemned to a previous past.

Many Times

Many times I have trembled,
Like no other, at the gate of love.
Many times I have stumbled
Like others at the sight of love.
And many times I have fumbled
In my several attempts
To grab the meaning of this word
That no man ever utters,
But now the fair Ocean
That I used to know is painted gray
And the brightness of all Days
Now seems to be a fair game.
Fountains on private beaches
Are no more fresher than the sewer,
And as I wander across this dark abyss
With pitying eyes and a lingering rage,
I trampled on a proud Glory
Therefore I command thee!
Retract thy spirit from a glimmering decay
That I could commit my thoughts
Once again, to a heart, where love falters not.

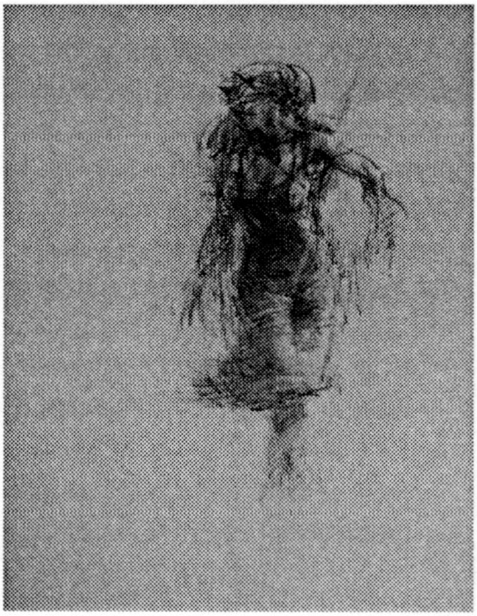

Homage to Loni

Be you a passerby or a visitor
To St Augustine on Miami Beach,
I guess, I dare not ask from thee
If you've ever seen my dearest Loni
A tall gangling lass with a head full of dark hair
All lolling in the air with a mused rhythm;
One that is full of a quiet but confident breath.

She used to call me soft names
At a time when I was lovingly harnessed
By the tra la las of a South Beach.
But I'd better hear her voice
More than any one else's.

I dare not tell you at this stage, that,
I might be asking too much of you
As I see no reason why every man
Should miss the sight of my dream,
Not yours, remember!

Never have I tippled over a drink or two
And never have I ever come across any drink
Better than those that She pours forth
Into my cup.
For they make lesser cups of others
At St Augustine's bar.

But with a toe hold on a slippery surface,
I guess, I dare not reveal to you
That, She's between the 2nd and the 3rd street,
Where a grey handiwork mixes with the shade

Of a historic building, might give away
The visual sense of appreciating my game.

I dare not bring to your attention,
The fleeting image of her lovely Henry,
A beautiful dog with a pretty appearance
That makes a joke of miracles
And of other handiwork's,

Neither will I tell you odious strangers
About the general appearance of my dearest Loni,
For her taste in dress overwhelms like a cistern
That does not only bubble and winkle at the brim,
But one that constantly overflows with style.

Therefore, for the preservation of my only delight,
I will save the lashings of my strenuous tongue
And the dilemma of a heart so sore
That it makes a native of my aches and my pains;
For the devils in this world and all over

They are always ready to slay and to devour
The special love of my dearest one, Loni.

Now, Reader, let the stranger in you speak,
Of nothing else but an honest truth, and tell me,
How do I fence and wall this Love of Mine?.

let me be your absent friend

Somebody's Collection

The world is somebody's collection,
Owned by a faceless stranger or a nature,
One whose true nature we have never seen
Nor the nature of its physical being.

His character we have never been able to decipher
And his structural presence we may never know
But the elusiveness of the owner of this Museum
To our own human nature means
We will always be found wanting.

This world as somebody's Museum
Has a life that is verily verily filled
With golden sun and its broken colors;
If we say the least of all that lives,

And amidst these mountains of objects - collected,
Lie the strands of love and the strains
Of other hearts. Those that were broken
With their burning grief and their previous desires,
Perched on mountaintops and vales below.

And in this inventory, is the World,
Inside which I am found wanting.

Loni

Long before the fortune of a browned out atmosphere,
was the stretchy band of a hot and roomy 'pheric'
noon;
another space you cultivated for us, under the sun
and another state that was some moment ago, –
frenzied
by the raging quivers from a molten orange

those quivers, that were shot to earth
as the glowing hands of another noon song,
for it to be cited and recited, by all, at a time when:

Only you, could provide for aching hearts;,
with your warmth and your dulcet tone.
only you could provide for ailing hearts,
a faultlessly perfect song and a cushy comfort;
one that beats the glowing hand from the other noon
song.

only you could provide for longing hearts,
at a time when others wish for nothing else
apart from those that are wrapped in the traditional
mind:

about time and its transient moments and about a state
that could never be roped nor held together by pieces
of strings,

Never has a tenuous time been measured, before,
by the quicksand's of reality or by those of fantasy,
nor has their ever being, any system – so devised,

that one could stack up the streams of time,
with those that are wrapped up in our minds,

like those quivers shot down to earth
as the glowing hands of another noon song;
one whose fabric you 'Loni' have personally set

In your own terms. every minute that I may spend with you
becomes inestimable to me, and if it becomes possible for me
to pinch the personage of time and release it from its immediacy
and from the hold of feelings, then, I am sure certainly sure that:
you will be nowhere but there,

when our good heaven's feelings for a minute's minute shall be wrapped
in the millions of mild but mutual fund of a passionate space,
that you have created and cultivated under this sun,

and I and I shall never ache for any comparative other.

let me be your absent friend

Was it not

Was it not my selfish self
Who dared you to?
Or do you take it as life's design?
That I, a poor artist; to whom
Bread and cheese seems
To be, a boundless treasure,

Could preach none other than
Words, born of pessimism, that
One day, nature's strength shall decay
And all superficial beauty shall resign
And fade away.

Now, this same self, proposes
To teach you love's sweet lessons.
In the hope that you may;
In your lifetime, open your heart
To a love's most loving employment…

let me be your absent friend

I think I would die happy

If I were to die under her steady gaze,
I would have died a happy death,
And better would I have felt
Than a player-less fiddle without strings,
For there will be no one to half my joy.

But like the Biblical thief at night,
A silly bastard stole my only love
And the Pavements my feet used to know
Suddenly becomes a strange-way.
The concrete terrain that I once loved
Now seems a fair game for marauding rodents.

So if I were to die now,
I am afraid I might die scowling
And maybe scare the comforts away
From the nature of natives of heaven.

My fear is that you've forgotten
The stubs of my unshaven beards,
The tough muscles of my manly butt,
And how those cheek bones of mine
Used to congress with yours.

So if I were to die now,
I am afraid I might die scowling
And maybe scare the comforts away
From the nature of natives of heaven.

Let me be your absent friend

Please don't honey me anymore
For a powdered rose is never a cure
For the broken hearted
And neither could it be a substitute
For the loss of the other.

Your eyes might have bore within them
The greatest power I've ever seen,
And I, in my naiveté, could do no more
Than to fix my lively hopes on them,
Without knowing that our sideways glances
Will never be more than sideways glances -
One that is never strong enough
To keep you away from the temptations
Of a crowded street.

And now that you've allowed a silly burgher
Into my only space, I can do no more
Than ask like a gentleman would - from you,
That from today and other days,
Could you
Kindly dismiss me from the service of your thought
For the glories of our perfect days are clashing
And our uneven thoughts can no longer be same.

Please let me be your absent friend
And you won't have to honey me anymore.
Let my love lie still and slumber
And maybe in my wake
I shall see more clearly than before.

A powdered Rose

How I wish I could kiss an angel
Since the silly Saint has warm lips,
But it's the flapping wing that worries me
For my lust might be blown away
Like a beer's bottle top, and my heart
- exposed to thirsty wishes.

A strange name and a strange e-mail
Was all it takes from an old foe and friend
To tear the fabrics off my thoughts,
When I thought my thoughts were no longer
Being ensnared by the pouting nose of a Fox.

But then again,
I, being consumed in my flight of fancy
Felt the need to develop a protective thorn
For the protection of my paper-like sandals,
Whilst passing through these thorny fields.

I, with pen, dressed in non-murky ink
And blind texts, activated and actualized
Like a sand full of thought-full footprints -
Of things said before. Whilst those unsaid
Will forever be committed to memory.

Even now, when I rage with anger
And a certain controlled trepidation
That a Foxy friend (Elena) never calls - anymore.
I therefore write this little note,
To a friend who went for a bit of a paddle
In a family nest, and left behind, a powdered Rose

let me be your absent friend

And a scent that will never deter advancing rodents.

Now that you have left this sun-soaked beach, with
Another of your powdered Roses, left for other days,
Never let the touch of a Mum sleep by your passionate-
Care, for what is truly yours, has got to be by
Your own hands, grown.

The last five lines is my way of spelling NANCY

I long to know about my Childhood past

I long to know about my Childhood past,
But not from my mother's passionate tongue
Or from those laced with sweet treasures
That pour forth from a father's tongue.

I long to know about my Childhood past,
As it pours forth from someone neutral
And as distance, as the blessings of the sun .
Is to earth.

For then, I might know who I was?
And why I am what I have become today.
Maybe the question 'why' in my humble life
Could then be answered once and for all.

I long for someone to tell me, of my innocent years,
To tell me of that time, when I was most vulnerable,
And about that time, when responsibility could never
Have been mine whatsoever, for my actions.

I long for a reliance on others, to access the unknown,
For the true nature of the unknown is like my death,
And like my death, my infancy is beyond my
conception.

I've always known, that I will remember dying,
Like others, if and when time comes bashing in,
And mostly of all, if heroic circumstances permits.

But before then, I command those that know
To please tell me what my infancy was ever like?

let me be your absent friend

Was I ever a lousy bastard like all infants?
One who keeps the mother awake all night?

Now that I stand out as a diamond geezer,
And one given to charming the birds. Tell me,
Had I ever been one, given to wet nappies?
Did I ever stammer before I could talk properly?

With a raging anger and trepidation!
I remember thee my country, as my home...

I

The mornings at your gates of promise, I remember,
For I was lucky enough to witness your youth,
And your upbringing, whilst your brick foundation
Was still fresh and full of the workman's breath.

On the banks of Unity and Faith, I remember thee,
Standing with your back turned against a unitary state.
I remember how you henceforth shed your Britishness
For the colorful garment of a sweet singing republican.
Now your breath is stifled by greedy and greasy grits,
And from your mouth comes a cloud of harmful air
One that I could see, painted with the decadent colors,
Colors of debauchery, indulgence and imperfection.

Such is the honor of your scars, that,
I bore your stigma like another displaced effigy.
But the lid has been lifted and the bins cleared
To unleash my labored tone and a poetic anger
That runs through my heart, like a Saracen dagger,
Therefore I shall not feel sorry to publicly state
That, your unfettered lust and negligence
Harnesses nothing but vulgar decorum.
And your image no longer fits its embroidered borders.

II

Maybe Man would have been perfect
And so could this World have been, – perfect,
If our Lord God, hadn't taken a holiday.

let me be your absent friend

But God, resting and lolling about on the seventh day
Has robbed Man of the perfection it truly deserves,

And this seventh day complacency
Reflects more on none, other, than my Home.

Therefore, I see no reason why, I should shy to recall,
The memory of a supposed to be 'father land', my home
Where its leaders are full of sweetly recycled phrases
And the arsenal of those managing this 'Eden' of a place,
Can never be seen – drained in daylight,
Or to be seen relieved of their recycled promises.

But if God had worked on the seventh day, then
The labors of having a vision in my own Home
Would not have disrobed truth (if any ever existed).
Illuminating bulbs would have not been punched out
And loads of promising dates and their talents
Would never have been jilted, wasted and raped
By those same leaders – to whom navigating wrongly
Seems to be a common template.

Maybe if God had worked on the seventh day, then
The kitchen of the so-called bloody leaders
Would have yielded or provided good food.
Labors of good citizens would not have been wasted,
And many Innocent Angels would have no need,
To hold their fires like Demons, on the sideline.

But since God rested on the Seventh day,
This home, like most homes, has never been a place
For our dear hearts to lie in.
And its playing grounds have never ever

Possessed a room (big enough) for our use.
We've fallen out of grace, and
We've fallen out of worldly favors,
And our thoughts, made us strangers.

Therefore, I have no remorse, whatsoever,
For thinking about my Home – (my Country)
With a raging anger!
Even in my silence and in my trepidation,
Its complacency and its unfeeling,
I will always carry with me.

III

There comes that time in the year
When everyone is proud and happy
To think kindly of their own home.
But what could I think of a home?
One that has condemned my thoughts
And discarded me to wander in my prime,

Therefore, why should I not address you?, my home
In my sworn silence and my trepidation
Why should I not remember Her, still?
For putting into practice, those channels
That made a stranger of my thoughts
Ever since I was born.

Her provincial landscape I still recall
Her past glories I would always recall,
Her wasted potentials, I weep for -
Piles of which I and others alike
Could never be wrongly accused
Of speculating on its loss, and my homelessness.

let me be your absent friend

That Pandemonium set the axe loose
Before the Camel's neck was ready,
Was never my responsibility to bear?
But here is my poor soul, wailing, moaning
And suffering from a prescribed displacement;
That was never by my hand molded.

So, I see no reason
Why I should shy to recall,
The memory of a supposed to be Shelter
In the most disenchanting tone.

IV
There is enough provocation – already, in the world,
And there is enough duty laid on imagination,
But a fierce and an unpitying home,
Raped and re-ordered my nature
Along with others and their pitying mode
Now, your Sons and your Daughters
That you once blessed with stern refinement,
Are scattered everywhere for others to see
And to use steadily and as a whole
Whilst You, our supposed to be Home
Remains affectedly deaf and unfeeling
About our experiences and about why and
What makes us speak this way?

Therefore I have no remorse
For silently thinking about my country
With a raging anger and with trepidation
For Her memory will never die in me,
And neither would God's complacency

On the seventh day be forgotten.

V

Like the fortunate few, I have tried
From places far away from my own home
To draw a portrait of my only known home
Or what used to be my first love.

But this popular anger in me,
Is rough and is ugly. It stiiiiiings
So bad, that a diagnosis would be useless
For no prescription on earth could better
The painful portrait that this thought gives.

VI

At times,
I find it necessary to mix the moment
At times,
I find it disturbing to correct odious memories
By necessitating irony and slipping into the unexplainable
But new accent, new experience and new problems
Renews a sense of old that refuses to be forgotten

For my Home will not die in me
It's walls, as borders to my memories,
Is nothing but a haunting specter.

VII

It is out of love that I loathe thee, my Country,
It is out of love that I do bemoan thee, my home,
As your plain, and unfeeling evidential status
Rips through all that is of others and me alike.

let me be your absent friend

That I've chosen this medium to commend thy shortcomings,
Should not be taken as my foulness of mind,
That I've chosen this platform to praise your Kurskian nose
Should not be taken as bimbling through a non illuminated path,
For only the power of plain speech could rethink,
And maybe amuse, whilst revealing the quaking habit
Of a Home's wall - charged with its own tremors.

Therefore the odor of my Home
Or what is left of my Country,
Is a non-redeeming charm.
It is one that hurts and haunts memories.
It is a lone specter that hurts all senses,
And if you dare share a measure of my experience,
Then, this charm, I believe will haunt you.

'Another day', Africa

It's almost high tide now, and the poor fisherman
Laboring hard in his paper thin fishing boat,
Could do no other, than to rest his line
And resign his fate to a promise of 'another day',
For the rising tide of his present day (one that he knows),
Has left the ocean parchment, clean, clear and dry,
And the ocean lives that he think he used to know,
Now lives a clustered existence, in the bunkers of his mind.

Yet the nature of your love, Africa, is not for once withdrawn,
From the everyday quest of the poor fisherman's,
With your breath, you filled the poor fisherman's line,
And brought promise and grace to a clustered run.
As it pleases thee, Africa, you revived his nature with grace
And the twilight doom that used to be, before,
You, Africa, changed and filled with the promises of plenty.

Death and Decay is no longer the fisherman's maiden name
And neither was it by choice or design, designated
To board his ocean, his line, and his paper-thin boat.
Now his line, warbles from the blessings of your nature,
And the blooming song, of a spring-like harvest, filled
His gracious voice, like the tensions of a resurrected mystery-
One that was rescued from a doom and a deepening shade,

As no one else could enrich, and restore what seems dead
Other than your presence, and the nature of your love, Africa.

let me be your absent friend

Now

Better than ever, was my vision, now, that
The tides have come and gone,
And hordes of hours have passed you by,
Yet the rays of a longing evening sun,
Left the brows of your eyelids - fresh and strong.
The hands of the evening sun, have been
Lodging away, from its native domain,
It might have been strong enough
To make others cringe, but its presence,
Left no shadows beneath your eyelids
And neither does it show a drooping trait;
Around the muscles of your lovely lips,
For the muscles of those kissing lips
Are still as fresh and as strong as ever.

A lone Rose

How could I for once in a living moment
Prefer to ignore a lone Rose,
Sitting and seething for being unsheathed
By the waves of a sandy South beach,
When I know that deep in my heart
I could do more than needed,
To water and to nourish – this life,
And another, to live,
And to even prolong another flowery existence.

Marian Piety

I
I am desperately seeking Maria
One with whom I once rowed
Over a rib

Nature might have made you different
And set further your putative course
But your adoration in grief
I do share
For it was no choice of your request
Neither was your agreement made optional
By the same hand of God
That made your submissiveness permanent

II
Failure and Providence on God's path
Once drove Hagar into the desert's heart
With a son to tender

But for you Maria
The success of your piety and grief
Will always be wrapped in cotton
Stained with unjustness, cruelty and indignity
Like your own garment

III
I must admit that
I sing more of your piety than praise
For you have shed more tears
Than any poor soul

I must also admit that
The weight of your tears
I no longer carry in my soul
For mine is a fake dignity and pride

Whilst Magdalene's dignity will be
For ever purer than mine
And like the subject of your passion
Her tears would forever avert
The best of minds as 'he hath determined'
(Judith 12:04)

IV

So am I desperately seeking Maria?
Or simply another wet-nurse!
Or am I seeking a crying wolf?
One who's current of torrid tears?
Would wipe this pretentious dust
Away from the surface of my heart.

The Flight

Often She stops – more than twice
In Her destined but hasty flight
To breast feed Her only Child
On her motherly lap.
A single, unmarried teenage mother
Who in her hasty mood, lives
Droplets of Her God-given milk
Trickling down Her infant's Cheek
Whilst it innocently suckled most
The "bread of heaven"
As given by a human heart.
In Her unpretentious but hasty mood
She leaves traces of her footsteps
With droplets of splattered milk
Embedded in those "rocks of ages",
But who is "weak" and who is "mighty"?
In the face of Herod's sword and banners,
Who leads who through a "barren land"?
With Herod's army in pursuit, and
Who holds who with a "powerful hand"?

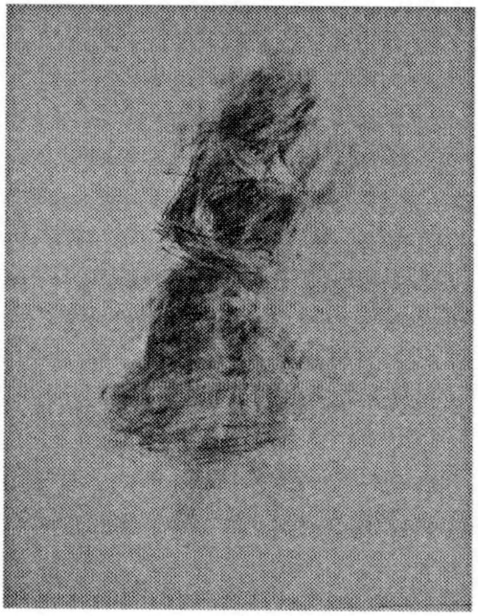

let me be your absent friend

Stains and Blemishes

Stains and Blemishes inherited in our days
Are none dressed, other than by light removed.
But perception and memories of our time
Are not by light dressed or removed
Neither were they by light recalled
Sadly they are by fashion determined
And so are images of our Gods and Angels
Like light, they are by nature deceived
And like love they are by dubious intuition guided
Therefore was image by nature condemned
Or was our nature by image deposed?

Save no tears for me

On the passion of Jesus, I tread
Between Gethsemane and Calvary
And upon His I left my footprints
That no prayer could be saved for me
And that no tears should be shed for me
Except wailing songs of human woes
For what is to be will always be

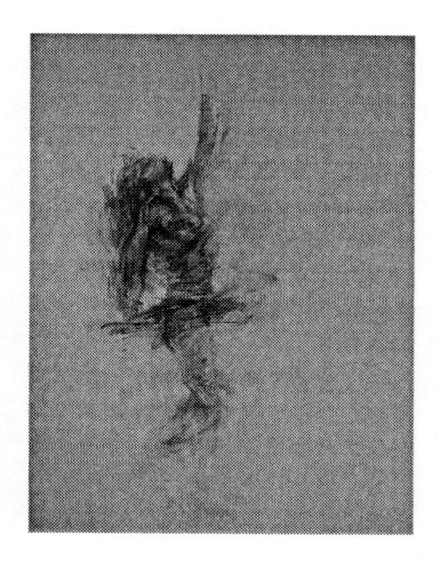

Your love on my conscience

Maybe I should feel great, and
Maybe, my spirits should be high
Knowing that your love
Rests firmly on my conscience.

Maybe I should agitate a bit, and
Maybe, ask about what I have done
To deserve such an honor
Of a love's dependency

Maybe I should speak out, and
For other ears might help to describe
An objects of assumed confidence and self-interest
Or why love and loneliness were virtues

Africa

I listened to your song
Whilst you were here with me
I listened to your rhyme
And the strange words we spoke
Everyday and every night
Whilst you were here with me

And it was the truest music
That's ever gone into my ears.

Now that you are gone Africa
The memory of your rhyme
Mounts upon my thoughts
Like strange words
Creeping up a strange wall

As the music in your absence
Was different from before.

Despite your physical absence
I still talk to you inwardly
And spoke the gentle words
That you thought me
Whilst you were here with me

My empty hands I held out many times
Shaping and groping the air
In the hope that you might be there

Several times

let me be your absent friend

I twiddle the chord less air
In the hope that your song
Our song will never be broken -
Halfway and that our feelings
Will never ever be lost
To this distance between us

A perfect danger

After several messages unreturned
And several promises unfulfilled,
I wonder why I still feel
The tender touch of your palm
And the tender touch of your skin
Burning between my upper arms.
Perhaps,
I have become too used
To your usually soothing breath
Drumming and drilling into my ears.
Perhaps,
I have become too familiar with
The contemplating base of your feet
And the sideways gesture of a head
That you artfully dropped to low
To congress with my left shoulder.
Perhaps,
I have become too used
To that even smile that you invented
And that soothing vocal chord
That only you perfected in a manner
That embraces more than a doves.
Now,
I could think of nothing else
Other than to seek a perfect danger
Of my own heart desire…

Timbuktu

It saddens me to discover that
Even a pearl is no longer fit
For a humble Timbuktu
Who like a mother heritage,
Raised and fed you all
On balanced diets of Knowledge
Whilst others were still in the dark.

How could you claim to be,
What you are today?
Whilst the great mother Timbuktu
Remains a theater of clay and wood.
She sits in her rustic glory,
With her faded freckles of gold,
Dusty and sun baked by its past.

She carried on her face and within,
Mapped lines of learned compassion
Striated by public pain and neglect
That only She alone, now bears
As the shadows of our time
And it's stinking political garb
Prefers to ignore her, for her suit
And the historical dusts in her wake.

It might take a while
To bring a smile back
Onto her face again.
It might take a while
To get her back
Unto her feet again

For the hands of time and
Left her no tributaries.
And those of ungrateful bastard,
Like you and I
Left her heart broken.

Great mother Timbuktu
With her lack of green hills,
Was liberal in her days.
She was there for us
When we needed her most,
She provided for us
When we needed a good start

Yet her fabric we've ignored
By standing outside the shades
Of her illuminating shadow…

Viii 2000 Miami Florida

let me be your absent friend

une architecture decouverte

Contrairement a la voiture decouverte,
Je ne sais pas une architecture decouverte,
Jusqu'a ceci moment de folie stupide;
Quand du monde son presqu' englotir.

Unlike that of the open car or cabriolet,
I have never known of an open architecture,
Until this moment of silly madness;
When the world was almost engulfed.

We skipped through the Primitive, into Neo Classicism
And we've oscillated, when it suits our needs, most,
But why do we deform in order to reform -
One and other likeness, that we've done away with?.

Strange feelings do have its own strange benefits,
And human minds, will always be wise enough - to sense it,
But, could the past in our present be created wrongly,
For the oncoming present, to be forever wronged!.

Arcadia was, before the Moon, we were told, and
Maybe, poor pre-antiquated Arcadians, lived
Next to the Creator; with nature, in perpetual darkness,
And all, substantiated elements - still in consonance.

Images, today, unfolds before my eyes,
Like a step, back into neighbouring history;
It bears not, the burdens of past Arcadia,

And it portrays not, their beastly sorrows,

But, degrees, of re-creations, it portrayed;
Severals, that are dissonating to fresh minds,
As pasts, in their presents, were unjustly painted,
By past neighbours, like Monsieur Poussin et Watteau,

Who; in Flippant Issues, of an Arcadian spirit;
Portrayed as sweet, poetic, heroic and disciplined,
Allowed not, a tint, of genuine pastoral sorrows,
For, their veritable Passions, has been Latinised.

That, the period of Jupiter, reeks of beastly existence,
Has never bimbled off, from pages of events, it is here,
With an invigorating rapture, enlivened by Bulgarian jokes,
About the latest Architectural Language, in the millennium -

Of Cabriolet Houses, lolling all over the Balkans landscape;
Where Sympathisers, are free, to experience a roofless Arcadia,
Pretend!, to be a Primeval Savagery, and seek for yourself,
How primitivity, reveals a redeeming feature plus other benefits

If you can torch-up, your place of abode, this coming Winter.

Oxford, England. UK (July, 1999)

Every Woman

Every woman walks her way
Whilst every Man judge their sway
They called it holding the sway
At a time when wiggling sideways
Was most effective for minds to sway

Some take delight in it
Whilst some relish judging by bodily gifts
And how hard blessed it is
For a red blooded Male to critically judge
Who looks right and who looks the clumsiest?

But all agreed that
Most times the clumsiest
Is the most daringly inviting
With all the delicate parts
Clearly accentuated

Miami Beach, Florida. USA (May 2003)

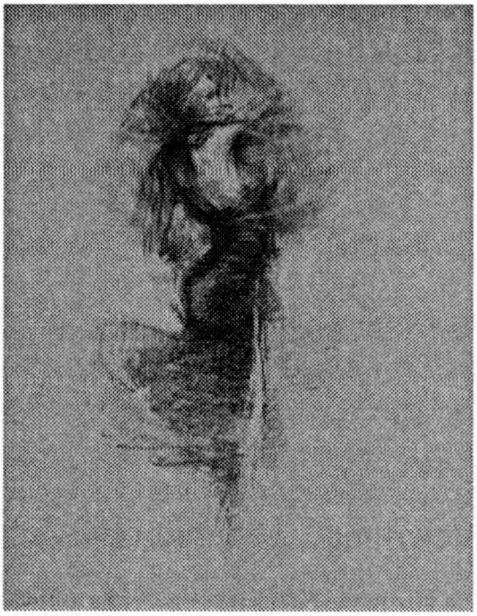

Pain when hooked

written as a compliment to an article about the ethical treatment of animals in the <u>New York Times</u> sometime in the first quarter of the year 2003

I

The slag tide provided the mother fish
With a humble advantage, below the pass
And the she thought it, a better time
To give lessons of life, of living and of survival
In muddy waters, to her young ones
She called out in the waters and gathered them
Like Soldiers, she halved them around her
And quartered them afterwards "for better
Coordination" she says. She warned them
Against "dangers from the Anglers
Hooks and fishing traps, otherwise you'll
End up on someone's dinner table"

All through her life
She had never hid her dislikes for Anglers
For Anglers, to her, are a bunch of bastards
They'll cast a line; they'll hook a fish
And will think nothing of the pain caused
And inflicted on the poor fish, struggling
For its survival and for its life that is
About to end at the other end of the line

So while swimming through muddy waters
And keeping out of reach of angling fellows,
The mother fish led her young ones
In an arrow head formation, with designated look outs

Covering her flanks. She taught them to look for
Fake bugs that sputter about in shallow waters
And those fishes that are not really fishes
Sensing danger at being spotted by Anglers,
The mother fish instructed her young ones
To change formation, by spreading out
Some Anglers took aim, shot and missed with their nets
And with the best part of the tide on their side,
The mother fish led her young ones to an RV point
Where she took it upon herself to check,
To counsel and administer to the needs of her
Shocked young ones.

And before moving on, she taught the young fishes
About the dangers posed by the stars above
As anything beyond the water world
Is made to cheat them of their prized freedom

II

Though rattled and concerned for safety
And the future of her precious young ones
The mother fish, took a final glance
Before approaching her final rendezvous
Knowing that her anger at Anglers
Will always be an effort in vain
She hoped, one day, the shelter of her grave
And those of her precious young ones
And their bones will never have to be
In the bowels of …

Those bloody Angling bastards
They said fishing is fun and hooking – a sport

let me be your absent friend

Yet they won't hook their own
So if they won't do it to a loved one!
Then why do it to a poor fish?
Why inflict pain in the name of sport?
To the other life at the end of the line
Why celebrate a period of discomfort?
And a certain type of pain caused
And inflicted on another life

We might have been cold blooded
For our own survival in these waters
And our nervous system might have been
Wired differently from other beings,
But poor fishes, like other animals
Do respond to stimuli
And do feel pain when hooked

If the human world is a civilized world,
Angling should have been a participatory sport
Wherefore all concerned should be made
To catch and to quickly release
Precious fishes and other captured life
Back into the waters where they belong
So, silly Angling bastards would no longer
Celebrate the period of discomfort, caused
To poor fishes by dispatching them
Into their plates via the grill
Maybe then, we could agree that
Fishing is fun

Miami Beach, Florida. USA (March 2003)

My true breath, I held

You are like a flower
The stalk of which I beheld
Within my right palm
Like Abraham's knife

Your green leaves I tenderly touch
With slight feathery touches
From the tips of my left palm.
Your freshly watered face
I slightly touch, as if it were
A weapon of desire.

But you never knew
That I was covering up
My true breath

My sorrowful tunes
And my misfortunes
Of the past few weeks
I kept away from thy green face

My true breath, I held
Away from your presence
Away from staining
The freshness of your face

In the hope that
You shall never have to know
How much pain this pain gives

In the hope that

let me be your absent friend

You, my precious little flower,
Will never be made to loose
Thy freshness, nor wither
Before thy God's given gift.

Miami Beach, Florida. USA (November 2000)

If I have to write my mother, about you

And if I have to write my mother, about you,
I'll write to tell her about your sideways looks,
As if I'm writing about a dark Maria,
One that now resides permanently in the alcoves
Of her only son's heart.
I'll write to tell her about you
As one whose heart is the warmest
And who kept me away from her hold.
But what should I say of your charming smile?
That it has made me overlook my own self,
What should I say of your dulcet tone?
A voice that charms better than millions of angels,
How should I describe your stance
And how you take your paces?
What should I say of your nose?
That it is better than Cleopatra's....

Miami Beach, Florida. USA (November 2000)

Sorry

Sorry,
I walked away from you
Because I did not want you
To see my sorrow,

But
The painful memory of leaving you
When you've ever been so nice
Haunted me day and night

And
I hope you will in your heart
Forgive me
If I should say that, I love you.

Miami Beach, Florida. USA (November 2000)

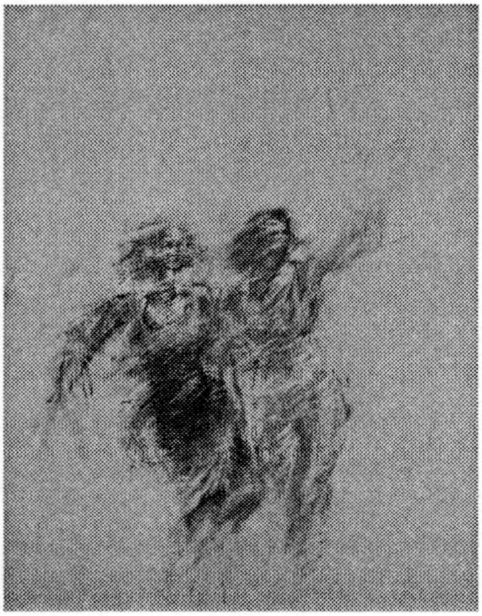

The Cat fighting its Claws

As gentle as the direction of the flame
Whose course was changed, by the wind
As the wind made its presence known,
So too were the paces of a one-time alley Cats
Now bent on presenting a remolded self
As a house Cat and as a cultured one,
Loved, bathed, parted and well shampooed,
Much to the envy of the Claw
That it wished to divorce itself from

As if there is no slugging issue to bemoan
And as if others idea of progress lacks
Momentum, the Cat realizing its own presence
And its own commanding interest over others,
Stretched first, before opening a Catty mouth
With a set of clean catty indentures,
Before letting off a Catty sound –
One that was to signal a beginning
The beginning of its case as to why
It has decided to fight its own Claws

I am a Cat the proud Cat said and had been
A Cat now, for two months less than a year
Not only am I so proud to make this count,
And not only am I so proud to make this claim,
So also are others that I will name in this case
But before that time arrives, I must remind you
Once again that I belong to a family of Cats
And a lineage that is far older than Moses

Pausing for a couple of seconds, the arrogant Cat
Took the opportunity to look at all listening
And after measuring the effect of all said so far,
The Cat without mincing words, went on and said
Proudest of all Cats will I ever be, as I a Cat,
A one-time alley Cat, now a house Cat,
Stand here before you today, wish to remind you
Good fellows that all through generations
We, I mean my family of Cats,
Have always performed our duties
Just as expected of us Cats
And happily most was I, a Cat, when I hopped
Here and there and into other places
Happily most was I, a Cat, when I jumped,
Twist and turn like most Cats do –
To stress their agility over others

But my life now as a house Cat
Is one that is ready for a change
It has been touched by that change
And other affections that come with it
And as I do not wish to dwell on a part
Or be enslaved by the same part,
I therefore thought it best for myself and
For the interest of the part involved as well
To act by dissolving our co-dependency
Type of relationship
Like in all relationships, this decision
Has not been an easy one, to make
For, doing so, means, I, the jewel of all
And the prettiest of all house Cats,
Shall be seen to be divorcing myself
From the barbaric tendencies posed by the

let me be your absent friend

Ever presence of a Claw – my Claw

And if I am seen to be moving away
From the presence and the thinking style
Of the Claw, dearest Ladies and Gentlemen,
I'd love you to see this as a move
To unburden myself and rid myself
Of an outdated gift imposed on me by nature
I'd also love you Ladies and Gentlemen to note
That it has never been my way and neither
Will it ever be my wish from now onwards
To go back on my words. For as a gallant Cat,
I have never believed in pestering an old Love
With flowers, nor do I believe in clustering
The grayness surrounding an old Love's grave
With dead desires. For dead desires,
When laid to rest, should be allowed to enjoy
The company remaining out of lights favor

So I though it better in my interest and those
Of others, especially the interest of my new friends
To simply deny my Claw - a loving flower,
From causing an injury to a loving hand
And to rescue us both from becoming victims,
Growling in the field of a no longer loving hand
Hence my Claws, as I see fit from today
Are no longer worthy of my worldly desires
And neither do they – my life's desires
Anymore. I can live without them
I have graduated from being an alley Cat
Into a house Cat, and now considered myself
Blessed by God's grace and all comforts given,
Here and within life in the house.

Yes, it is a change and a step forward
And to most conservatives – I guess absurd
But as made known to me and others
Within my line of Cats
Being able to graduate from an alley Cat
Into a house Cat, have its own private demands
Its responsibilities and its public expectations,
I shall not attempt to grade as benefits,
Nor will I ever have it dressed in those ranks
That falls between the parties of drawbacks,
Of limitations or even prohibitions
Nevertheless, I shall and will remain true
To my presentation of this case as it is
In a socially true life
The demands and the expectations, placed
On a Cat's progress by its simple merit of being
A Cat, I will suppress for that of a universal
Idea of providence to reign the most
And this, I hope shall remain the focus of all
Jurors, following up this play of issues
As it affects the nature of one life
And another life's advancement

I shall start by highlighting what we all know
That every cat and their Claws were by nature
Bonded together.
An inevitable marriage it seems until now
When I, a Cat got caught in between the nets
Of providence and progress
And rather than live a life turned both ways,
I, a Cat, a one time allay Cat, now a house Cat
Have decided that, for the rest of my Catty world,

let me be your absent friend

I would sleep happily, forever and always,
Knowing that I gave reign to the notion of
Shedding natural responsibilities – this time
By surgical means like most people

Questions of what was discovered by the Cat
Or what was waiting to be seen by the Cat
In its ascension to the top of the stairs
No longer fits into anyone's line of queries
As it has been made elegantly clear that
The quest for a search and the need to improvise
Has been somewhat made adaptive but not
Quashed by an old establishment –
One that takes its pride in repose,
A tradition set up and a well-taken road that laid
Waiting for the rough grace of an alley Cat

And after making possible it's only wish –
Becoming a native of another's world
The alley Cat moves into the house,
Sheds the garment of the underworld,
Developed a taste for the high table
And for being finger fed by a new owner
Yet, it refused to educate its Claws
For as certain advancement comes with
Certain benefits, and certain benefits
Like better things in life
Are private and not for all to be shared
As better thoughts are better refined
When solely conceived,
So also is the way of this Cat

Reason is

It takes more than a couple of strides
Across the face of longed for stairs
To make possible a longed-for journey
But now the aim is completed
And main objective achieved,
I, a Cat, could do nothing more befitting
My status, than to shed my garment
A Claw, my Claws
Claws that make old the previous
Before it soils the present like a past
And as I do not want to be reminded
Of those days when it was necessary
To slug it out with Rats
As most family of Cats are known to
Therefore, in the presence of all,
Ye lovely fellows in this court today,
I, a house Cat wish to divorce
An unworthy Claw and discard it
Like you would an old shoe

But at the hint of an attack from within,
The Claw, being sharp and always focused,
Refused to be out performed
By the challenges looped into the court
From the hands of an enlightened pretender
So the Claws from the paw of the Cat
Emerged, made its own presence known
And like a blade drawn within a bunch of grass,
Or grasses, stressed its case
As if the struggle for a peace
And a continuation is far greater
Than a freedom from ones guilt
And a dream of a responsibility

let me be your absent friend

That never was

I am a Claw, representing all Claws
I belong in the family of Cats
For they rely on me and my services
For their existence in this world
As you have just seen
I am angry enough to change my life
And I am angry enough to break out
For myself
And from a bonded routine
That has always been my life
I am angry enough to break away
From this edge and from this periphery
As I'd rather be buried alive
Than to live a lie in a painted life
Built on thresholds of opposites
And pretend as if
Tomorrow will be a better day
When I haven't been made ready
For a total demise of the present

Happily most was I, a sharp Claw
When I helped the Cat
Twist, turn and hop and hop
And help execute many a painful
Entertainment - on the part of its preys
Yes, I helped make many a victim
Of a Catty lust, and a Catty dream
I made true, over and over and again
Now this Cat that I, in my scratchy ways
Helped make a Cat, has graduated
Onto a domesticated stage,

And I guess the likes of myself – a Claw
And our family of Claws
Could do with a better treatment
But rather than being educated
To adapt
Like my buddy – the alley Cat
I, a formidable Claw have been forced
To fight things out in this manner

I will hold my ground
Even, when being a Claw
Makes me the terrible one
That could only scratch,
Graze and tear
I will hold my ground
I will hold my ground
For the sane world needs
To know that even a scratch
Fellow could nibble as much
As the fellow could crop
So as a proud Claw
Representing the fate of other Claws
I do strongly protest in this court
That all Claws should be dearly
Educated and allowed to assimilate
Like the Cat, rather than being
Humiliated and discarded
Through surgical means
As it is being suggested by this Cat

Unlike this ungrateful animal,
I implore all considerate fellows in this court
To be rational with how we've all evolved

let me be your absent friend

In our different lives and like this Cat
We must not forget that
Life of the whole was made possible
By those of their parts
Even as fashionable interests keeps clashing
Its thread remains the thread of a true life
And the thread of a whole
For it is only by it that we shall be defined
As whole before being in the character
Of something strange to our nature
A Cat will always be a true one
And its state of existence will remain a true one
If decked with all its natural entitlements
Untrimmed Fangs, Whiskers and Claws

With these in place
Then I see no reason why all Claws
Would not love to be there as a quiet companion
When Humanly required
We want to be there for comfort and for warmth
When Humanly called for
We'd love to be assimilated into this new life
And do whatever gentle duties might be required
Of us Claws – graduating into a new life
As then and only then can a true life
Be accounted for
I could do no more than to impregnate
An already pregnant case, the second time
And this I will do by promising that
I, a Claw, would not be a danger
To the gentle human skin
At any given time

I love life in the new as well
But have grown not to envy it all
I could have loved this advancement better
And maybe put my resentment up a bit
And smear later
If the hand feeding of the house Cat
Could stop and made like it has never being
For the Cat is getting fatter and grotesque
And its brains becoming lazier by seconds
And I as the basis of its survival
Feared more for a rusty life
I can no longer condone its weight
And neither can I stand its wastefulness
When other Cats are busy flipping things
But if this annulment goes through
I must warn you lazy Cat, that
Any attempt to live without me
Will reduce you to nothing but a Toy
An invalid, in Human hands
You will no longer be a Cat
And you will never be seen a Cat
You will be fat, inactive and overweight
Imagine your life as a Clawless Cat
Living on weight watching foods!
Think of what becomes of you
A Cat that cannot climb walls

Anyway I have no great stories to tell
And neither do I possess the tongued power
Of an elevated presentation
But in the manner of truth and fair game
And not so highly flowered a taste,

let me be your absent friend

I, an ordinary Claw present my case
As best as I could
By doing so, I hope I have rescued myself
From being snared off the gains
Of a sweet world
I hope I have done enough for a friend
And more than enough to remind a buddy
Who aimed to live life without it Claws,
That in life, living without us – Claws
Will make you mild, meek and weak
And in the face of other Toys
You'll never be considered fit for a gift
Talk less of the cause of a Human weakness

I will withdraw into my place now
And before I do so
I challenge you for the last time
To please tell the listening world
How you hope to scratch yourself
Or even cover your shit
In a world of naughty Humans –
You are life, by and within itself
And you never want to stop
And look before the moment
As the carriage of an enjoyment
That you have become enclosed in
Failed to reveal that its fleeting side
Is its true nature at its best
And whenever it runs through life
It carries you along
As best as you remain with it
A passenger and a prisoner of
Fashion

In a world that sees you amongst others
As often stretching and purring

Your furs and all
Might have been allowed
Into a Humanly crafted world
Whilst you in your reality
Will remain bordered
By your rank as a Cat and
The hypocrisy of your action
Go on divorce me
And lets see how you hope
To remain a Cat

Miami Beach, Florida. USA (February 2003)

let me be your absent friend

The Pilgrim

I

I have sworn to the ways of a Vagabond
And placed myself within the reign of a Pilgrim
I go from here to there and
At best as the heart I seem to please

Like a skillful pilot, I withstand all the storms
That made my way its path
Yet remain forever indebted to my heart
In the hope that one day

My itinerant toil shall surpass its pace
And my heart, walk behind me
With the blinking lights of sunny days
Flashing to my command

II

But to my surprise,
My heart made me a Vagabond before a Pilgrim
And now a parting farewell will never be to my style
Neither do I wish for one too many from others
And those tongues…

That I wish their superficial beauties, arrested
In their mocking gowns
Even, if through the light of my days,
I have been seen, walking, and walking

Away, from my front door…

III

And with a back forever turned
Away from my front door,
And away from my own home,
Off I go,
To seek my heart's desire
Trusting that my fear
Is wounded and weak

IV

So, if Demons ride the whirlwind, as they say,
Then, it was their madness that brought me fourth,
And it was the same madness that tells me,
That I do not need the thread of a belief in my heart

For so long as I remain confident in my own company,
Then my fear is, and will always remain wounded and weak
In its own company

Miami Beach, Florida, USA (February 2001)

let me be your absent friend

Reflections in Maine

Yesterday was summer
And the moment, like all summers
Was spontaneously dressed

Today is winter
Whence footprints in fair weather
Force dampness out of dry snow

Soon tomorrow will be spring
And merry flowers with jolly ambiance
Will spring forth and blossom

With their colors, flourishing
Before their passion
Overtake our turn

Their death and decay
Means more to a continuation
Than it is, a perishable end

And so shall the spirit of the Artist
One who painted roses
To enliven other's mind

Whilst his own mind
Remained bitter
And his bank balance, empty

Moody Beach, Wells, Maine. USA (June 2003)

let me be your absent friend

The greatness of Death

I give praise to Death
For its elusiveness to sight,
I give praise to death
For keeping its dimensions
Known only to itself
I give praise to Death
For keeping its personage
Beyond all senses
And for keeping its strides
Infinite and measureless
For knowing the personage
Of Death,
Would have lessen
Its value

Oxford, England. UK (June 2000)

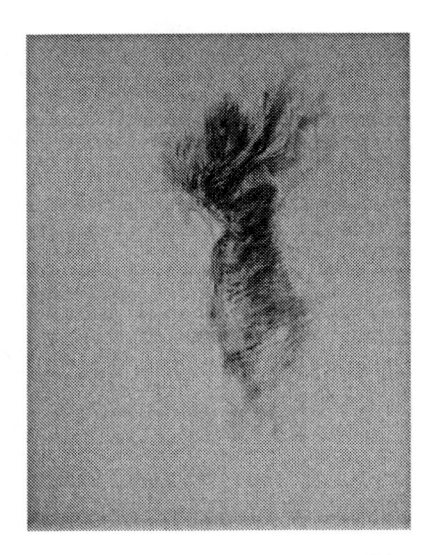

Monica Lewinski

I see the woman
You were born to be
And pretended
The other one
You were painted
To be, never
For one moment
Existed

I see the woman
In you…
Struggling for light
And you
Like a fresh plant
Trying
Not to be crushed
In a manly world

When the beauty
In you
Was degraded
And the life
You were to live
Was deprived
Of richness
By the other

That circumstances
Placed on you

let me be your absent friend

Though many
Will not believe you
And many still
Prefer to pretend
To hate you
Whilst they secretly
Harbor what it means
To be covertly

Clintonized

And in a land
Where all realities
Were once but dreams…
You, only you, Monica
Had the guts, to thread
Where others have failed

You actualize your wishes
And took the blame
For a coffee glass
That sweated
Where most glasses
Won't

You took the blame
For a coffee glass
That left in its wake
Traces of traces
On watered rings
Upon which you,
Your glory and pride
Resides…

So
What can you do?
To be
Once again

Miami Beach, Florida. USA (May 2002)

let me be your absent friend

Going Greek

There was once a time
When the God's really flourished,
The only thing that distinguish them
From the living was a revered fear
And a reasoning that was privileged.
Then, along comes the age
When the Gods' were going cheap,
Unshaved bollocks and unshaved beards,
Smelly armpits and lousy dress sense
Thus become their selling point.
And I for one refuse to buy,
Cause I was so cash starved
Attention never got paid
-in cash.

But the petals of Godly reasoning
Did not drop like a feathery stone,
Freeing itself loose off a sandy stem
And young leaves of Godly passion
Did not gather in Temple stalks,
For it to be autumnly dispersed.
So, could this be an Athenian Temple
That I see, set before my eyes?
Could this be a mirror of a broken past
That I see here, there and everywhere?
Or could this indicate a time –
When the Turks were one shot lucky
Making tea bags out of Elgin marbles

As I join the chorus of visiting
Visitors…

Buckingham, England. UK (September 1998)

A note or two

Every time I read a note or two from you,
I feel a longing presence - all around me,
Oh! How I wish, I could for once,
Hold back the modes of livelihoods debt,
Give up my death under a starry presence
And vacate my one and only place
In heaven; if there is any for me,
Let alone, share my muddy grave
And my last possession on earth –
A coffin, with the lingering memories
Of an itinerantly warm Slavic breath.
Oh! What a promise, it would be, to note,
That I, accompanied with a Foxy breath
And maybe memories of waking up,
Every morning, in your loving tender arms;
Will not remember my own death,
Neither will I, my own decomposing state,
Nor the time spent partying with maggots.

Buckingham, England. UK (March 1999)

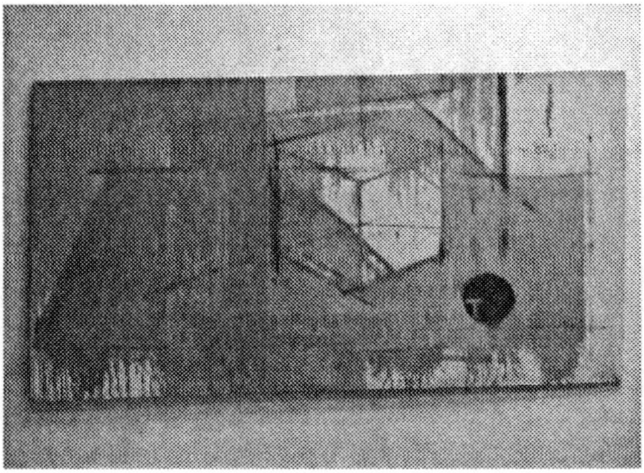

Idaamu Oluya

Never did I set out for the odd ends of the fabric,
And never did I set out to set a stage for myself,
But since this stagy core is dressed like a night
With subject matters forever clothed to occlude
Whilst true experience continues to evade all,
Then literary confidence is an Art that misjudges,
Its coziness – like doubts that inducts at will
And doubts, at times
Are not purely of truth perceived.

If ever I should fail whilst clothing the Arts with texts,
Then, my failure should be blamed on measured texts
And not for the unorthodox way – of the said and unsaid
Neither should it ever be about how it was said,
As products of imagination can only be reduced to texts
So far

Oxford, England. UK (October 1999)

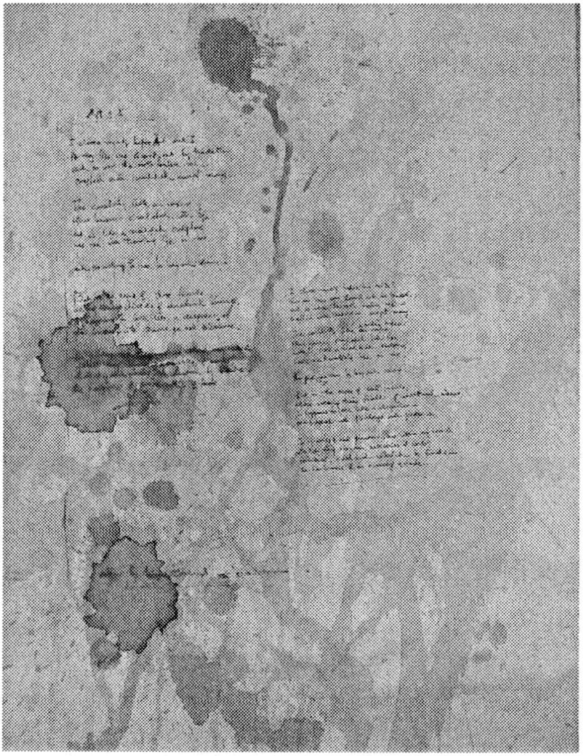

let me be your absent friend

The Carpenter's choice is better than mine

I still hope for an uncertain hope of progression,
When the Carpenter's choice is far better than mine.
The pedestrian quality 'useful' was my description,
As the Chimney sweeper's blessed with more choices
And more speculative expeditions,
Far better than mine.

Pride for the halved is in not being Arcadian enough
For Jupiter's sun to expose. And too uncouth be it
That is half fit for Praxiteles tools.

Like John Keats bleating little white Lamb,
I once cried a cry, for needs and wants implied,
But Atlas and Saint Christopher went away en vacance
Leaving the prolong effect of chin-kwag, chin-kwag,
On the muscles surrounding my chin, cheek and lips.

Now, do I get a sideways glance?
Or should I beckon for another maiden day?

Oxford, England. UK (October 1999)

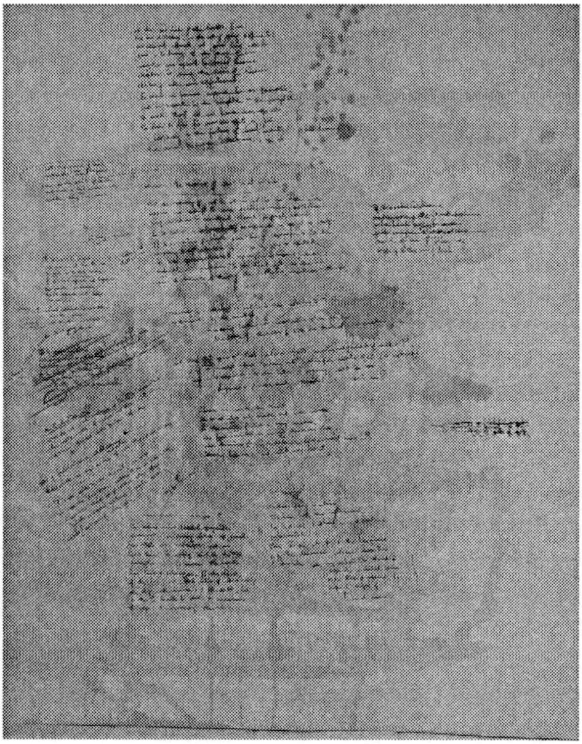

let me be your absent friend

Do not beckon for another maiden day

Do not beckon for another maiden day
Cause it's always better to read of a passage in life
With the other's life contract, left
Unstained and un-honored

Let your hopes and your passion
Be felled like that log of wood,
Sawed off its roots and left behind
In the woods, by the logger

And as the PC is to Apple Mac,
I am sure your hopes and passions -
Like the dried, felled log of wood,
Will someday be compatible

With the needs of warming up
Somebody's house in winter

Oxford, England. UK (October 1999)

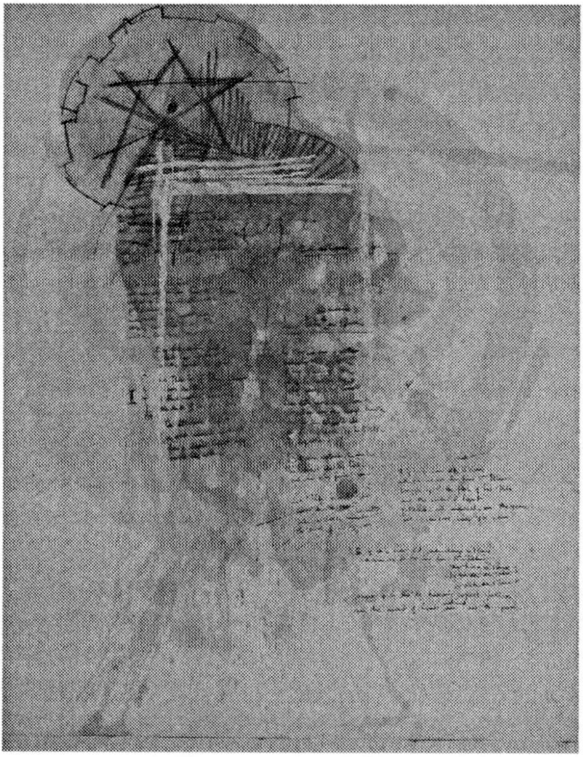

let me be your absent friend

Sometimes

Sometimes you look hard
Before you begin to see
If at all there is something
Worth seeing at all
And even when you look hard
You might not see a thing
Worth looking at all

The horizon in front of you
Hide those things you cannot see
As no amount of sunshine
Would reveal those things
You considered to be
Hidden treasures or those
Promises you considered kept
Which like broken Chinaware's
Were rather unkept

Miami Beach, Florida. USA (September 2000)

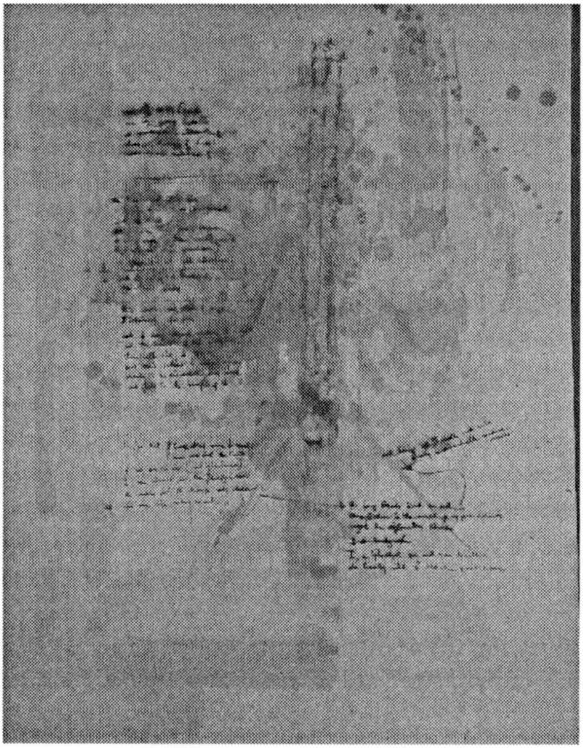

Some good things

Some good things will last forever
Whilst some good things, will,
With time, wither and fade away
Like summer, in Maine

But
The good memories of you
Will always be mine
To cherish and to care for

The notes you left,
I kept under my pillows
The memories of your footsteps
I kept warm by the fireplace
The tears you shed
I kept frozen as dewdrops
Splattered on a piece of silk

For I see no reason
Not to trust a friendly foe
More than I do a likeable friend
One whose smile will always be
Brighter than gold

That's why
The good memories of you
Will always be mine
To cherish and to care for

Miami Beach, Florida. USA (September 2000)

I hope it doesn't rain tonight
A song performed and broadcasted life on BBC,
London. 1997

Before the sun shines in June
The rain always falls in April,
Washing away old memories
And old images from our eyes,
But what happened to mankind?

Could somebody tell me why?

What have few people done to many?
With so many hopes floating about
Hoping some day things would change
And some day there will be hope,
But nobody cares anymore
Nobody cares for the less fortunate many

I hope it doesn't rain tonight
As I've got no shelter over my head
No tweed jacket to cover my body
From these injuries of life

I've got no love to hold, no love to hold
As I've got no shelter over my head

I hope it doesn't rain tonight, la, lala
Got nothing to protect my bleeding life
From this injuries of life

Why do people forget so soon?

let me be your absent friend

Images of cold winter nights
Images of people dying on the street
Yet nobody cares anymore
Nobody cares for the less fortunate many

I hope it doesn't rain tonight
As I've got no shelter over my head
No tweed jacket to cover my body
From this injuries of life

I've got no love to hold, no love to hold
As I've got no shelter over my head

I hope it doesn't rain tonight, la, lala
Got nothing to protect my bleeding life
From this injuries of life

I've got no love to hold, no love to hold
As I've got no shelter over my head

Croydon, London. UK (1995)

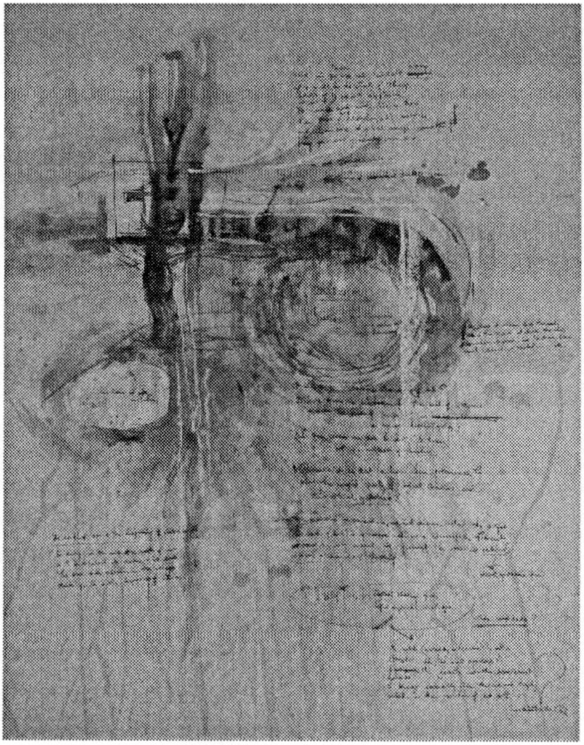

let me be your absent friend

Old Historic Houses

They once knew what grace was?
And what it means to be stately,
They are still around with us, today
And if possible – out live us.

They might have been made barren
And their hearts, by us, made feeble
But Old Historic houses!
Once had lives living in them.

The meaning of their grandeur
With lofty and dignified daily lives,
Might never be repeated again
And neither will it ever be exalted

Except by the intrusion,
Of petty eyes and of petrified subjects
That pass through
These Old Historic Houses

That once had Men and Women
Living in them

These Old Historic Houses
Once had Men and Women
Breathing through their walls,
With traces of all known vices

That used to live in their lives
Now left behind for some to study.

Oxford, England. UK (1999)

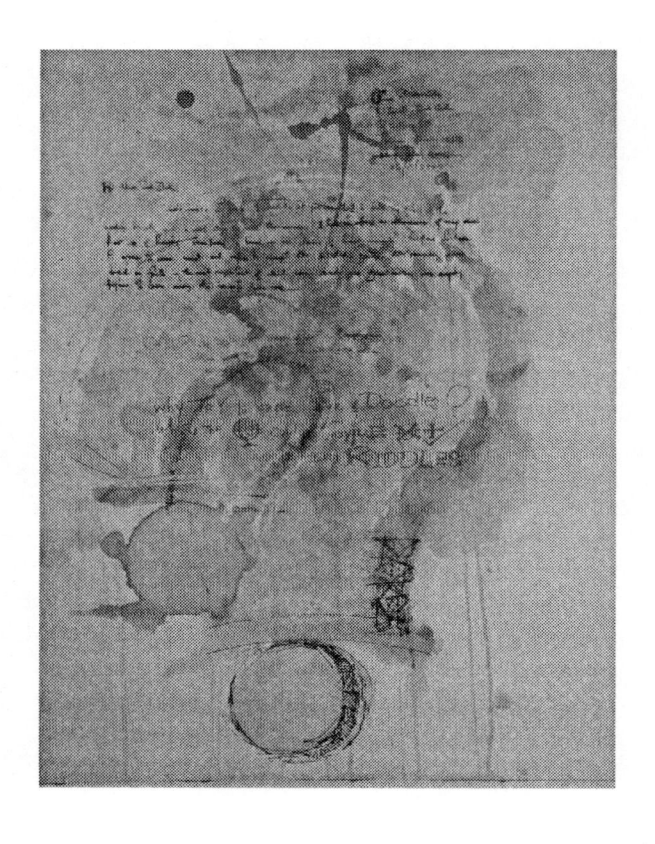

let me be your absent friend

A prayer for upliftment

To a cheerful Spirit
That leads a cheery life,
Make my soul a jolly one,
Devoid of pain and anguish

Pave my way to steadfastness
Full of life and heavenly delights
Adorn with bliss, for all to see
Through these shades of darkness

In a valley of dusty hues
Lies the soul of many a man
The rank and file of humorless faces
Shaded away from the glow

Of a pleasantly blaring sun
With passion betrayed and no remorse
And left to rot on a sable path
With lost minds and raped egos

So, to a warm hearted spirit
That leads a lightsome life
Make my soul a friendly one
Devoid of hatred and malice

Create in me, a neighborly spirit,
Full of love and heavenly delights
Decked in bliss for the sun to see
Amidst these layers of darkness

Croydon, London. UK (1995)

Before myself

My life was shaped out by tradition
And so were the roots before me –
All crafted and molded by many
But I choose my Art before myself
And true creativity, like a boiling anger
Thus become simulated with my life
Wherefore I, unlike a molded sculpture
Had one, but a trembling life in me
Now, nothing seems beyond solving

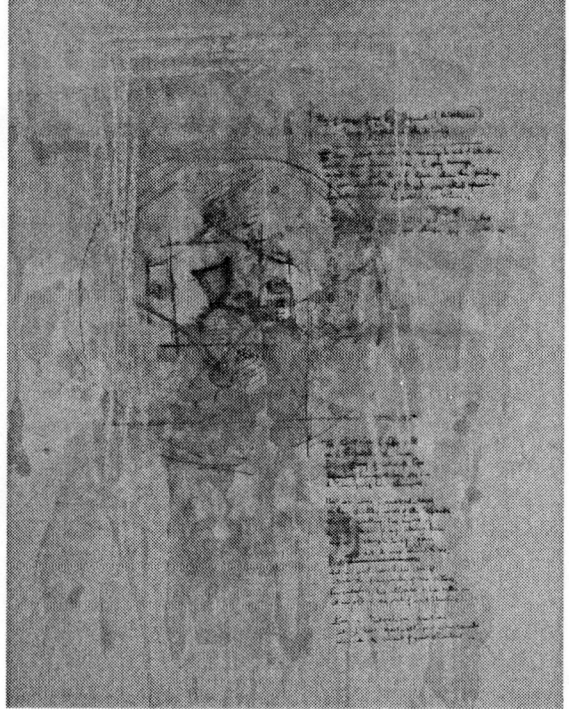

VSC Johnson, Vermont. USA. (June 2002)

let me be your absent friend

Kristina Sunde

I have seen many ionic columns in life –
All used to support a pediment
And the pediment, always decked with images
Denoting entrances of homes and shrines

Yet no one has ever decreed
That I should believe in images

Houses, now, in the modern sense
Are beginning to imitate temples and shrines badly
That it is now possible for a stone Mason
To be dubbed a Sculptor

Yet no one has ever decreed
That I should believe in titles

In your studio, I saw many paintings
All balanced confidently in their domain
And also well executed, by all standards
Yet you harbor your own reserves

That you are a drawer and not a painter!
Now, that has never been decreed

So how could you honestly account for your sweat?
And not deny those painted figures of yours
How could you abandon their trailing silence?
When capturing the nature of their character

Have always been within your limbs

How could you honestly account
For those bones, joints and muscles,
Captured, drawn and painted like no other?
The dexterity of your hand said it all

That you, young Ms Sunde, a Lady Artist
Should proudly pronounce yourself a Painter
And nothing else, for to do otherwise
Is to betray those figures

That allowed you to give rein to your emotions
Without becoming a Slave to your passions

VSC Johnson, Vermont. USA (June 2002)

let me be your absent friend

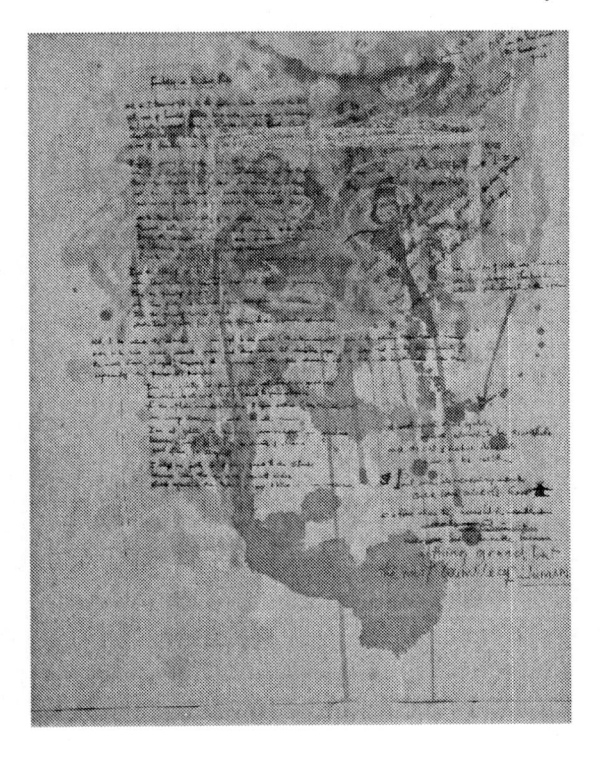

Moira Catherine Ferrier

We were strangers in this house
Yet my selfish self prayed for her,
My selfish self, prayed for her.

She was my strange design
And maybe my only intrigue
Sitting and swinging by her own accord
At the other end of the table

Yet my selfish self, prayed for her

That:
Soon the light will break upon her midnight
And the shadows of her beautiful handworks
Will soon triumph upon this scorched earth
At a time when the world believes that beauty
Could only be a compliment for the fool,
That a beautiful face could never get capped
With a beautiful talent, and neither does it
-a beautiful personality.

I looked through her feathers
As if they were those of a Nightingale
And I looked through her wings
Like the window of a known acquaintance
To whom being within a natural setting, means
Cooking up meals of bountiful creativity,
One douced with spices that only the cerebral
Could provide to the capable and able

let me be your absent friend

Yet the mixture of Roses and Lilies
Present in her journey through this life
Was never strong enough a tint
To beam the color around her neck
Through to the world, like a burnt clay

And my selfish self still prayed for her
That her bountiful talents, like mine, would
Seep through the shades of a scorched earth
Even when the world believes that beauty
Could only be a compliment for the fool

VSC Johnson, Vermont. USA (June 2002)

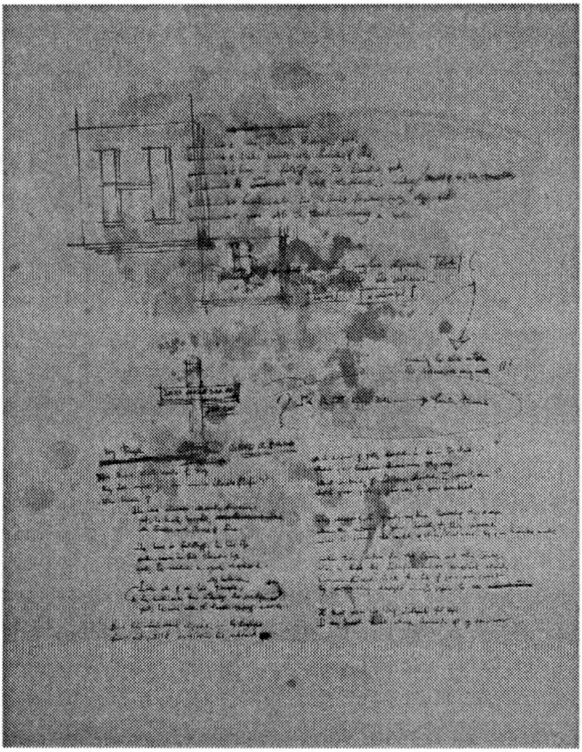

let me be your absent friend

Moira revisited

It all started as a table talk, as I remember,
And as usual, with demonstrations and questions
But I did not manage to move the chair
Nor lift the coffee pot over to the other side

The door presented no problem
As the light in the corridor –
Busy glowing but faintly diffused
In a world, with a mind like mine, afraid
Of leaving evidences and testimonies behind

This journey of some little distance

I was afraid of examining the ground
For fear of hurtling down the slope,
Pressing poor grasses, breaking flowers
And leaving traces on my way down
To maybe, nowhere, too far

I was afraid, afraid of a pain

The type that might be hard to conceal
And thus become too sensitively sensible
To nurse even a single word and many others
That could hardly be described as specific

I continued to hide under the professional
Whilst the development of the most private
I ignored and left to languish at a time
When the door presented no problem

As was the light in the corridor
Glowing but faintly diffused

VSC Johnson, Vermont. USA (June 2002)

let me be your absent friend

Nicole Peskin

The moaning wind said it all
As it swooped and sighed
Through the leaves of several trees,
As if exhausted by its own fury

Now there was an eerie silence
Preceding a bewitching hour – a time
In which Nicole Peskin moved
Like an elegant flagpole will

Through the gentle hands of time

Silence crept over and over
The sodden grass of Johnson, Vermont
As a bountiful amount of peace and calm
Was being peeled a the stormy nature

And your good nature kept its word
That, no thin branch, stem or a young stalk
Will ever be pulled loose
Before it's bark matures

Your good nature set it up
Whilst your conscious nature made ready
For any obligation that warmth, comfort
And hard work would bring afterwards

Your experience is your best gift
Yet you were willing to share it
With a total stranger like myself…

I could have been a murderer
Plodding through a brief interlude
Before pouncing on another prey
Like a sweeping light

VSC Johnson, Vermont. USA (June 2002)

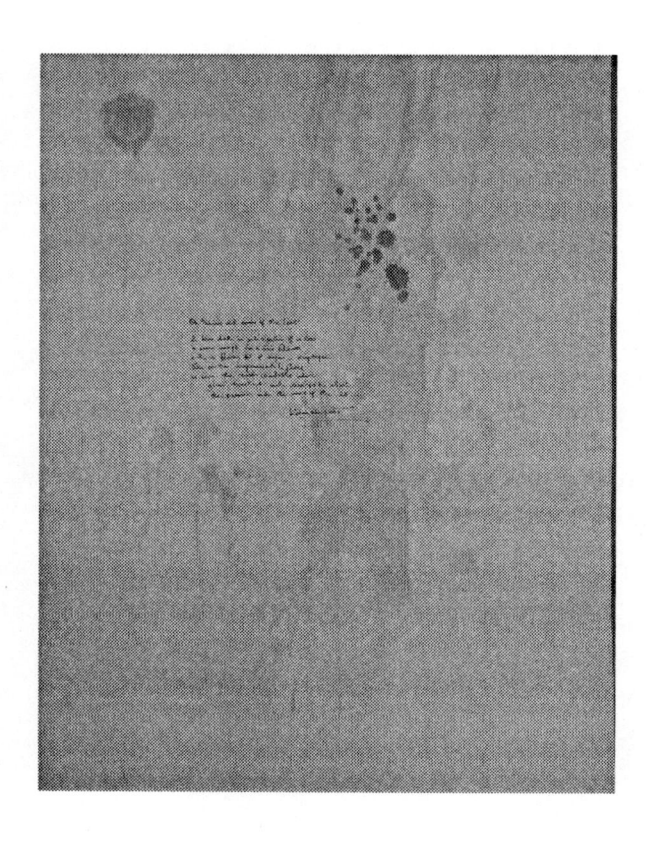

let me be your absent friend

Stacy Fisher

She took up stones in her hand, and
Smothered it with the most motherly breath
Whilst the world could only look and envy
The evolution of a molded wall
Evolving through the labors
Of her motherly breath

Thousands of years might have changed you
And your outlook towards life as well
But thousands of years did not change the world
For culture (regardless of your efforts)
Still remain wholly fundamental to the core
Whilst you and your sculpted deeds
Tread through its ever-changing nature

The freckles forming on the bridge
Of your nose said it all
And I could only hope that one day
You with your hands and motherly breath
Would be able to steer this fundamental ship
And set its able course aright
By charting anew – a course for artistic means

Then maybe we as Artists
Would no longer tread its nature
And the stains in our hands
Will no longer be a hindrance
To a status that we both deserve
As Artists and not Entertainers of sort

I therefore could do no other
Than to pray for your fingernails
To be able to hold more dirt
And for you to be able to eat with it
As well as dance to the sweat
Of your motherly nature of labor

VSC Johnson, Vermont. USA (June 2002)

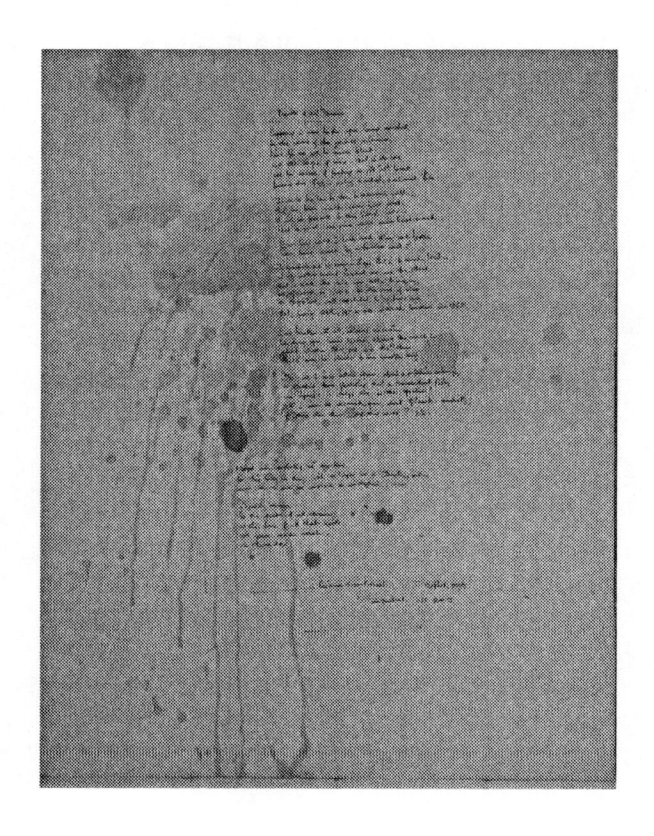

let me be your absent friend

Miss Buffington's music

I

The consolation of a noise in the circle of fifth
Could not have been made perfectly mellow
Had it not been played by Miss Buffington
And a commitment to a music enterprise
Might not have been made perfectly right
If our dearest Sammy (with a nice appeal)

Had not perfectly judged that:

Music, played within an Architectural frame
(even without its rigid structural frame)
Is good enough to be left – curiously unfinished
And good enough to initiate another progression,
-Away from the circle of lolling minds…

She played, for most, who could not dispel,
Hoping, that the best of her appeal –
Her music and her weapon in the field of
Ethical guidelines, will transform their taste

II

The stairway to the basement wasn't too bad
And the rows of square windows, made discernible
By listening figures, resting on a ping-pong table
All contributing to a blooming atmosphere
In which the colors and the shape of music,
Coming from the upright piano, reigned
And gleamed the senses more than the painted walls

The tune was undoubtedly moody,

Elegant in its lightness and grace,
Low powered by its delicate ascent,
Yet imaginatively balanced in its tracks
Like her playing hands

III

In your presence, Miss Buffington
Many men will talk in whispers
For the quality of your lines
And the grace at your fingertips
Has no place to hide
Than in others hearts…

Even when descants are rising still
And the scales on your piano remains…

The values from your fingertips
Will still come through
And beauty will no longer be still
In your hands…

Keep playing, Sammy,
Keep playing

VSC Johnson, Vermont. USA (June 2002)

let me be your absent friend

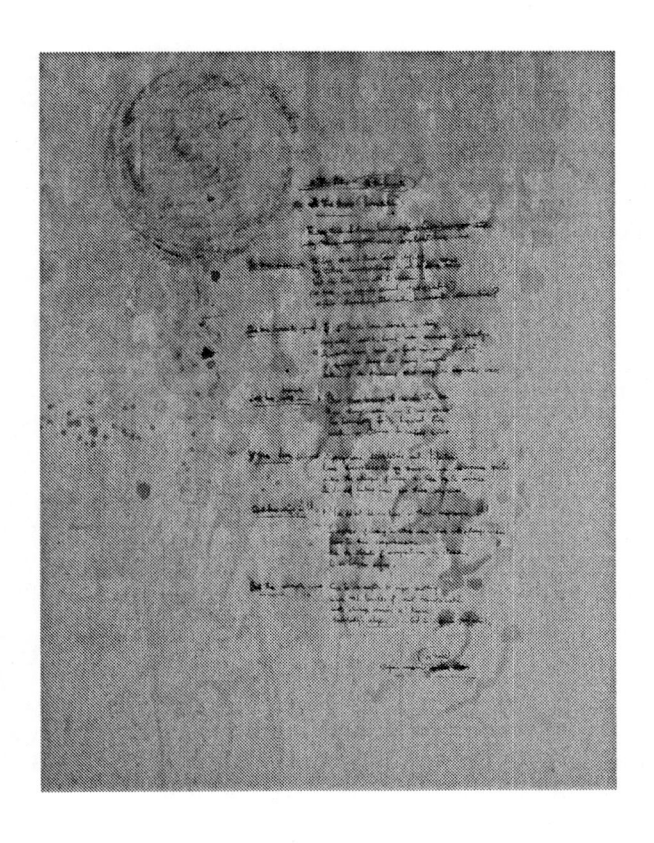

Feeding not grazing

Had I been a wise one, I wouldn't have thought
That you were sharpening your gripping skills and
Would not have considered it right that you –
A Cat might be brushing your teeth
An act that made many soiled and unclean
Because in this Human world of mine,
The grass is not a brilliant match for a Cat's food
And neither will the picture of a Cat grazing
Ever be considered - cool
Since it is not my way to shock minds,
I was never impelled to think beyond the obvious
Nor was I prepared to accept the obvious,
That a Cat might want to expand its dietary needs
By feeding but not grazing on grass.
For the idea of crediting a simple hygienic move
To an alley Cat, would turn a Human like myself,
Into the most formidable candidate for a pill-house
For grass, in this human world, is yet to be known
As a brilliant match for a Cat's food
Your voice, unlike most cats, was barely audible
For a gentle creature that nature made so articulate
Your state, was desperate as you were lonely in the alley
So I paused upon seeing you laboring hopelessly
With a scruffy looking figure, made shaggy
And un-kept amidst the complex array
Of sprouting green grasses, making up a sidewalk
But since the sidewalk presents you to me
As a subject worthy of my attention
I therefore commit my warm feelings towards, you

let me be your absent friend

As another life,
By composing these lines,
As moved by the gauntly looking shadow
Of an elegant form, now weak and barely skipping
For its life on the sidewalk

Miami Beach, Florida. USA (February 2003)

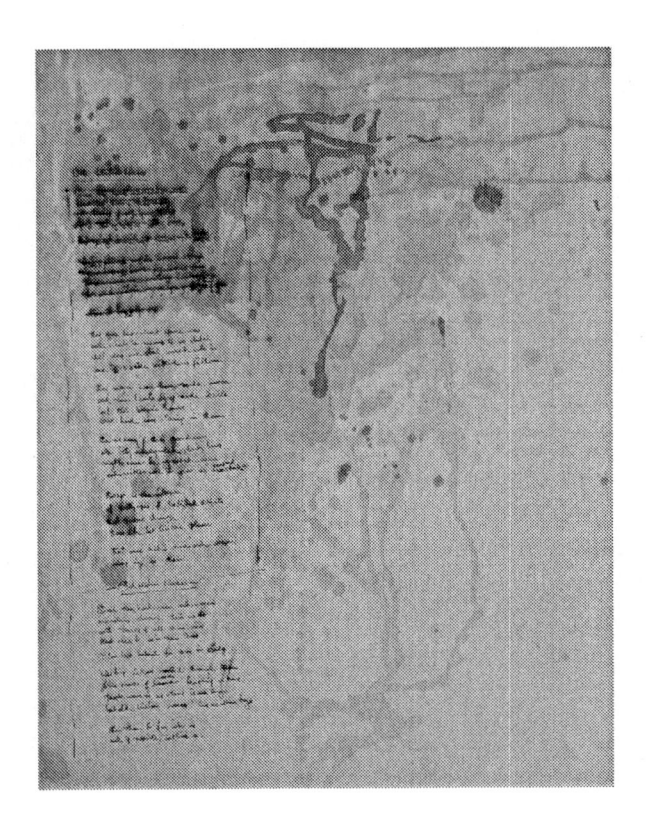

Judgment Day

On the Judgment Day; if there is any to come,
I shall tell no one, except the most inspiring being,
That I am an Artist and a Poet, but not a Sinner.
That I belong to those class of Creative Fellows

Those who spend their excessively imaginative lives,
Filling pages upon pages – of sketchpads and notebooks
With other people's misery, displacement and joy.
In my reports,

I will spare no Soul, and no Spirit will I ever favor.
I will show Truth, in its emphatic state of reality.
I will show the meaning of Pain - invested as Passion.
I will ignore Pity and apprehend material Characteristics,
I mean, ones that speak of Nature and of Nature's truth.

But why should I record and report my views?
Why should I be the eye of an inspiring being?
Why should I expose and ridicule living substances?
With hordes of time spiraling by.

Oxford, England. UK (July 1999)

Death of all Dreams

Supposing I were to die upon being excited
By the waves of the oncoming millennium,
Time for me will be forever silent
And this tongue of mine – that I do love,
Will be denied of feeding on its last breath
Leaving this stage in a dry, parched, swallowed state.

It will be bye bye to this burdensome world
That my tongue could never have loved,
It will be farewell to this horrible world
That a mind like mine could never have missed

But how could I have lived so far, only to die
Upon being kissed by a formless wind?

I created one too many – stages that I so much loved
While mother Nature created one and the other
That a mind like mine was made to live in,
But poisoned by Nature; was this mind of mine,
Its properties well copulated by Nature's own
That turning right left or even inclined becomes doubtful,

Living together with all, becomes uncertain
But dying upon being kissed, relieves the doubt –
About whether this one or the other
Could ever be so dearer unto my humble self

Oh! Will I ever bother again, about a relative average?
Or equating those qualities that a transcendent fixity
Was supposed to always give in this spectrum?

Will I ever be concerned again, about Planck's production
Of nothing other than conflicting waves? No.

Never and probably not anymore,
For this body by then, will no longer be a Church, and
Never will it ever be washed or worshipped again.

Anarchy beckons,
For the death of all dreams,
As the base of all that exists
Will forever remain rooted in paradox.

Oxford, England. UK (August 1999)

let me be your absent friend

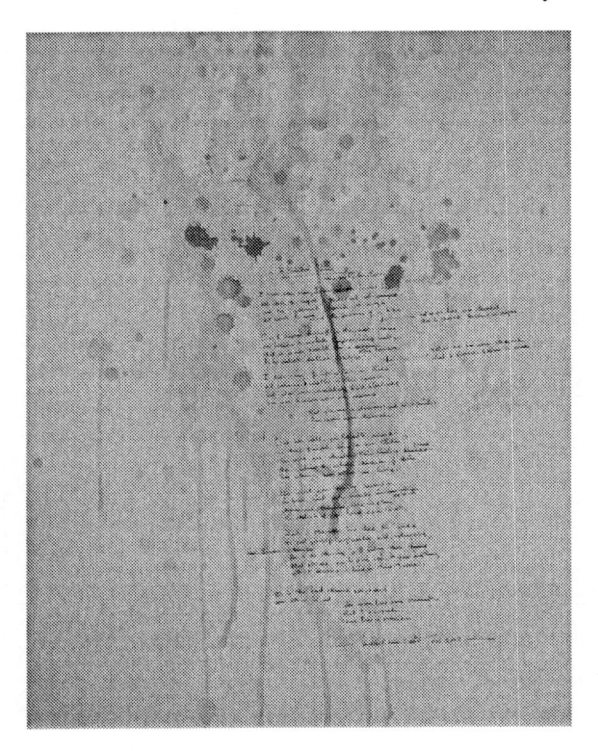

Christ Church College, Oxford 2000 AD

A Gothic looking hall with a busy skyline
Filled with sprouting vegetal stumps
that resonates its horizontal prospect,
Before its internal woodwork and cloisters.

A homogenous structure; whose façade
Speaks none other than of rich 'academic' terms
- simple rhetoric's and conversed knowledge.

History and Heritage and Tradition were thus camped,
And light, entrapped by the Jones's – an Inigo transom
With its monumental quadrangle, sculpturally formed
By the manly kind, of another Henry – a whimsical
Aldrich,
To whom rustication, engaged orders and pilaster
strips
Converge below a textualised but broken entablature

Which in turn supports a gable or a pedimental top.
Windows and horizontal symmetry are strangers,
As if Bess will forever be visiting.
Whilst the prodigious Logan engraved – a sweat
The sweat of those noble but evasive medieval masons,
With printed crenulations, with slim but punched out
Windows, to which we allude a steady evolution.

Such is its sweeter revenge on the viewer's eyes
That fragmentation suddenly develops a benefit,
Such is the richness of its historical contents
That empathy for its institutional consent

let me be your absent friend

Would never ever unite our thoughts, whilst
Its three-faced inherited character connects

The formidable with the intellectually suspicious.

The so-called revolutionaries revel in the suddenness
Of taste, of preferences and of vernacular interests.
That was humble in its conception but munificently
Decked in tawny colors of a Portland stone and others
In Oxford.

Yet, the humble-less visit.

They come in through the gatehouses, undisturbed,
That an epitaph-less Wolsey was not so opportuned.
Undisturbed, that the unfortunate Cardinal -
a Church's head,
Was even denied a common stone
to his unnamed grave
And neither did he…the butcher's son from Ipswich
Allowed his last possession – a coffin or a prayer.

Such is this Beckettian state of human lives
That visitors emerge from the college gallery
Lavishing the favor of their tongues
On the beauteous presence of the mighty
And the common. Depicted in shades of values,
And as arts, with their bequeathed status.

Such is its richness that visitors do emerge
Excited with memories loafing in fresher climates
As if memories are supposed to have wings
And as if notes of positive slanders – on tongues,

Do offer tunes that even passing strangers, now enjoy
The Leonardo's and the Botticelli's like a score.

Whilst I humble thou an a half folded knee
I, a friend and a persistent intellectual enemy,
Could resist not – the lavish but turbulent air
That was to devour the nature of St Friedswide,
By royal letters patent and papal bulls in 1525,
For bit of this and that in Christ College, Oxford.

A place in Oxford
Where articles, borne of longitudinal politeness
Combines the ruled, the ruler with an Ely-like taste
For a built but revered heritage of Christendom.

A Christ Church College, in the city of Oxford,
Where brains and breads – of humble hands made
Will forever help to fill the largest cook house
Before the cook house of minds.

Oxford, England. UK (March 2000)

let me be your absent friend

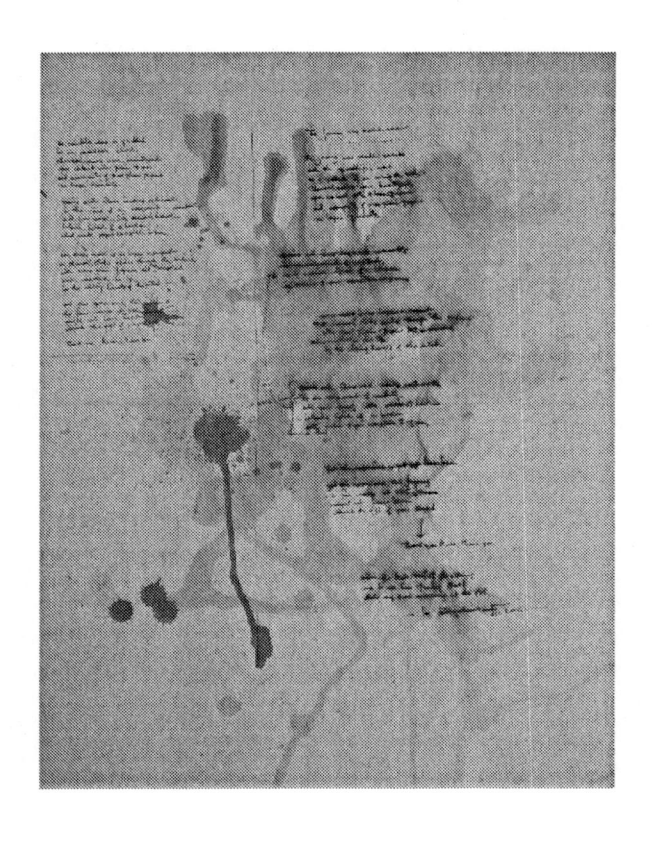

Buckingham

I, who once upon a time, departed,
Away from its shadows with a heavy heart
That was once set on Drayton's nest
When I cannot even beat a bush
In order to start a thief...
For bread and beef,
Buckingham bears no more.

Yet I unseen and not to be heard of
Crept away, silently from its serene hold
And away from its enterprising walls
Like that of Gethsemane's,
While she Buckingham remains
A sleeping beauty with its Lords passion,
Betrayed .

Your wonderful history I once surveyed
Your sleeping beauty I once weighed
Whilst you readily prepare others
For history, for chance or for skill.

But, are you still my sleeping beauty
With your Lords passion - betrayed?

Your noblest sorrow I once assessed
And your place as a village of mortals
Was not only with nature's decree
But also by providence given
That ye Buckingham like Gethsemane garden
Remains in envy of your gleams of glory.

let me be your absent friend

Though light and time have trampled your days,
Yet your nature, your skill and your patience
Was always your voice or your living treasure.

Your Old Gaol was a sweet peace
Sublimed, it bears a witness before you
And unto all others below the sky,
From when those Blakeian feet "in ancient time
Walk upon England's mountains green",
Whilst your refreshing stream, meekly goes in accord.

But for how long are you going to remain
The only sleeping beauty, whose Lords passion
Was once and twice openly betrayed?

That your mantle was once torn and shredded
Amidst wars raised by monarchs decree
And those of your Lords interests - surprised not.
For you have always remained between hostile kingdoms.

Your pride you seek through the lighted sandals
Of your Saint, the Ancients and your charters
While other kingdoms (left in the shadows)
Envy your dignity. But Robert Hill and others
Were proof that your importance was never
Assumed far beyond your merits
Nor was it ever usurped for your subjects
And in contempt of you neighbors.

Buckingham, England. UK (August 1998)

A Woebegone Song

When ones obstinate pride is brought low
And one can no longer assert himself, then
A crude response to almost everything
Within ones immediate surrounding culture
Seems to be ones most reasonable response,

The accommodation of meaning and interpretation
Of everything in sight, thus becomes conceived
With indignation and like another Blakeian job,
Blasphemy, Reasoning, Bickering and Cursing,
In the most caustic of tones, becomes one's response.

Then it will be easier to say, in one's flippant mood
That 'never ever! will a sorrowful tune be mine',

But do you really know what it means or feels like?
If all that could ever come out of one's pen
Is stained with Sorrow, Pain and Suffering
Or when a simple desire becomes foul
And tainted with one's odious thoughts!

Anyway,
The world of Job is in the book of Job,
It reeks of his suffering and his endless pain.
Because Job was felled by a hardened time.
As for his desires, he knew none than to curse
In order to elucidate away his sorrow,

And what is there for us to see?
An illustration of a sad woebegone song
Of protest motivated by a suffering

let me be your absent friend

That could no longer be endured, by Job.
While in the face of blameless and upright people,
He fervently asked

God! Why did you let this happen?

Oxford, England. UK (August 1999)

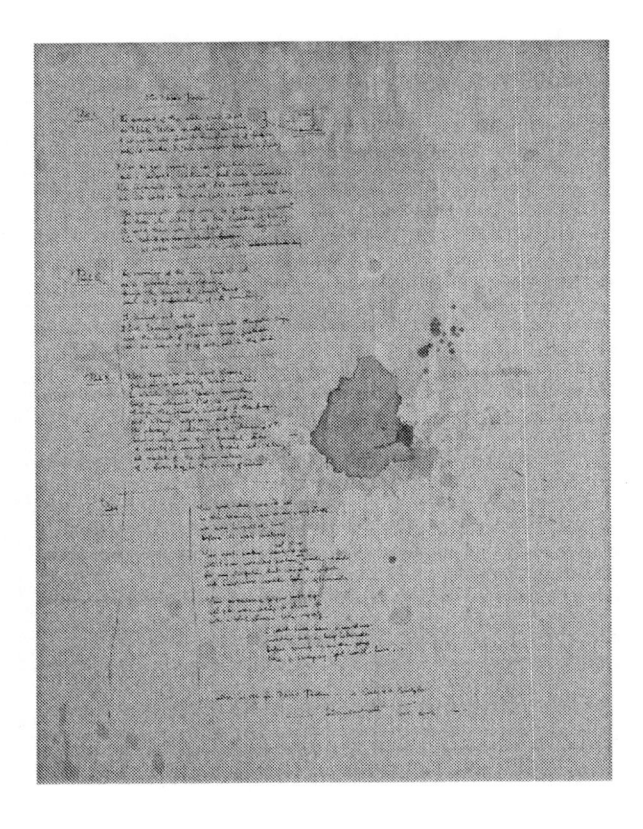

Last Breath

Funny how sweet you looked
When Death comes calling
And you in your last breath,
Smiled as if dying was great.
Your final gasping sensation
- said it all.
That Death at the driving wheel
Was after all a very gentleman.
He stopped and opens the door
- with ease
Whilst you, in your last breath
Hastily clambered inside,
Like you've always done
At Paddington Green station.
Leaving us to unravel later on;
How selfish you have been
To just depart so suddenly.

Many would have said goodbye
But you! you saved your strength
For the unknown journey beyond,
Leaving behind, gas bills, water bills,
Electricity bills and other bills
- all unpaid,

Your soul has departed this world,
For your body to remain earthened,
Whilst your stingy and miserly attitude
Was better displayed, by leaving it all
For others to pick up or loose all.

let me be your absent friend

It's even funnier to note, that
You seemed to have forgotten, that
Like every one of us, you came naked,
With nothing on you. Suprisingly,
You bid in your will like a wily burgher,
That you must depart in style.
Suppose every head is cleanly shaven
And suppose nobody smiles in heaven!
Then, of what need will it be to you,
Those false teeth and a bloody wig.

I must say
That you've taught me a great deal,
And I owe you nothing except memories,
Of which from now onwards
I will charge any friend – in advance
For taking their last breath in my arms.

Then I would have no cause to moan
Should they in turn save their final farewell.

Oxford, England. UK (August 1999)

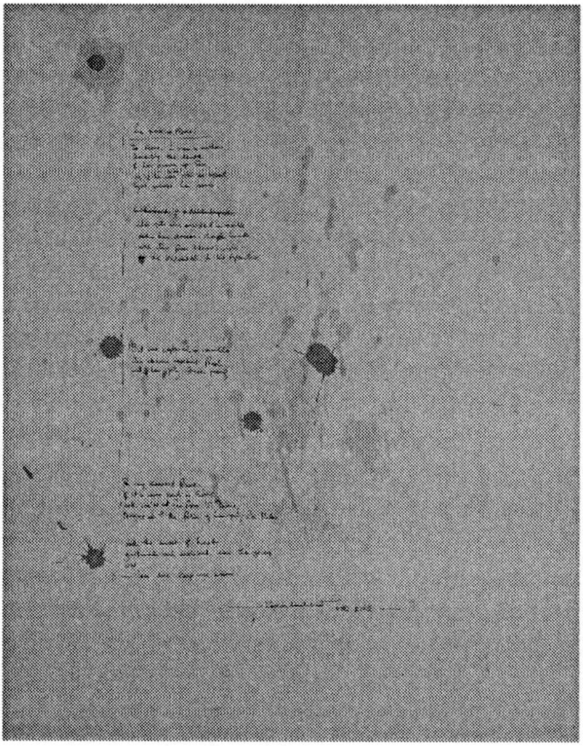

Some leaves

Some leaves have their abode in the air –
above human heads,
Where the birds and the bees
happen to be their neighbors,
And the stars were a distant next of kin –
far removed
From earthly beings.

Other leaves have their abode close to the ground
Where they humbly commerce with the ground forces,
In order to escape the wrath of a polluted air,
Only to find greedy fellows, conferring on their
personage.

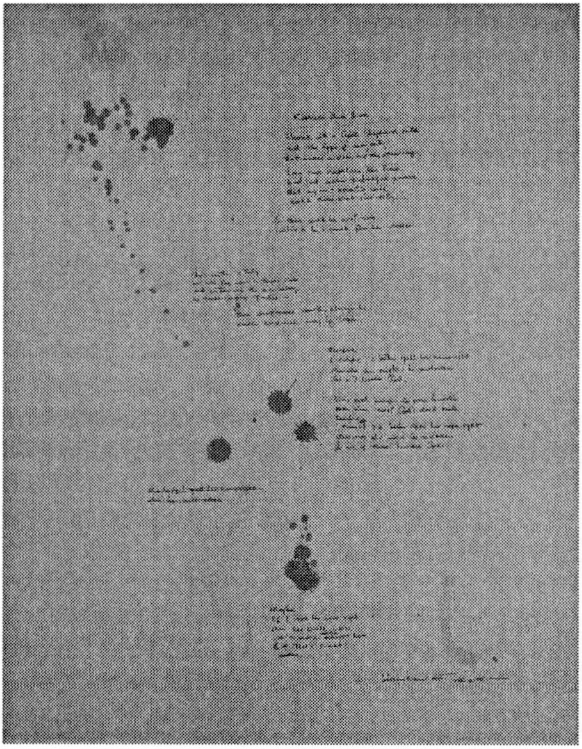

If I were to be a tree

Something along the ways of servitude,
Makes me think of the pattern of nature
As one at loss to humans' delight....
Therefore
If I were to be a tree,
I will be the most repulsive one.
I will have the patience of a rose,
For the patience of a rose
Never got any man very far.
And with the patience of a rose,
I would cherish my transcendental state
And would endeavor to never ever
Take any man, far from where he started,
Rather than bear the abused state
Of the patience of a tree.

Turning Tables

My dearest friend
Was it not your own silver blade
That cuts through your biceps
As if it was another melon
Wherefore your veins
Like the melon's nut
Were sparingly spared
From the cutting edge
Of the silver blade

Your pain
Though derived from a Failed reform
Was more of a protest than norm
And your own social discipline
Was no more than a corporate's
It becomes more personal than shared
More so
When a loved one turned the tables
Against the virtues of your bond

And you
Fearing all efforts – your efforts
Might be turned into a heap
Of waste – but good enough
For others to reap, as always
You forgot about the authenticity
Of pain and punishment
Regardless of whether both
Were by one's experience written
And painted in mind
Before being acted upon

let me be your absent friend

And you went ahead
To inflict pain as punishment
Upon yourself

Now, something
That started as a simple revolt
For moral consideration
Is in the face of all judgement
Helping out but not hurting
As the departure of a girlfriend
Is now beginning to reveal
Those manners of speech and
Those ideals of street allegiance
That only you could have suppressed
And hid from your friends

Your mind
I have always believed
Was only for high art made
And never for harboring
A friendly pain
But now I know that
The loss of a girlfriend's ear
Could sometimes be
To others advantage

I guess that's why
Girlfriends, when they choose to leave
(Their so-called Loved ones)
Do not always get blamed
For their actions

Nor those committed afterwards
By those they choose to leave

More so
Than that sharp silver blade
Should ever be than the force
- An alternative medium employed
And applied to inflict pain
On yourself (a Failed reform)

So, my dearest friend
Let your pain go away
When the last train comes your way
Do not allow it to drift nor grow aimlessly
As your mind, like most minds
Aren't directionally tuned
And neither will it ever be
Adequately equipped
To harbor pain

For Girlfriends and Loved ones
(When they turn the tables)
Will never get blamed
For actions caused
Nor those triggered
Afterwards

The knife should no longer be blamed
For cutting short a life
And neither should the club ever be
For a life so clobbered
As the bullet and the gun could never be
More responsible for a life

let me be your absent friend

Taken out, more than the force employed
By the muscles that helped
Finger the trigger

Miami Beach, Florida. USA (September 2002)

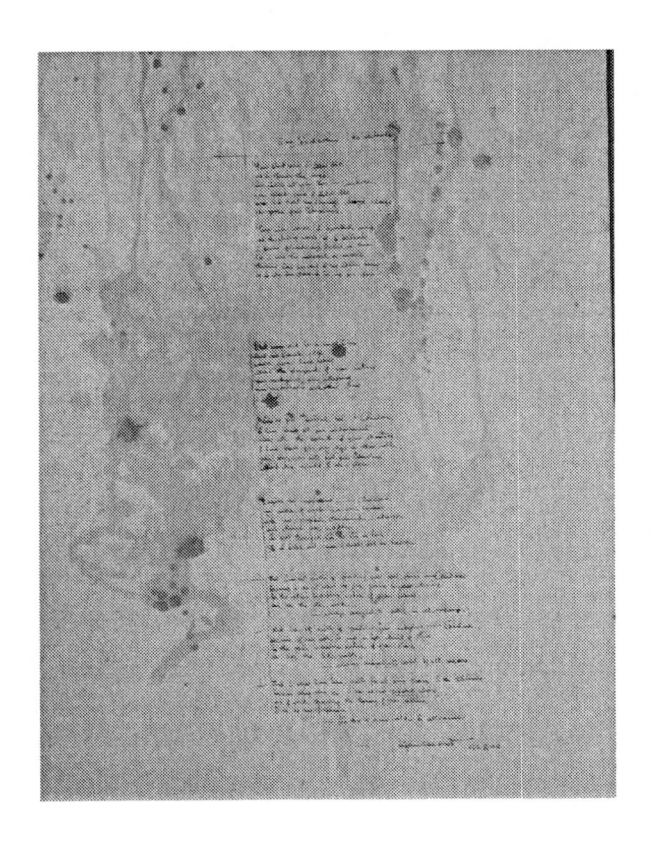

I have been a Child

All these years, I have been a Child
Sitting by the sea, with my ankles
Burrowed deep in sand
Whilst I watch others, at play
Unlike them
I refuse to build sand castles
And I refuse to gather shells
Cause I enjoy to remain as though
I was the only pebble stone
Left untouched by everything
But the sea

My gaze, I kept constantly on others
And ignore the waves as it seeps through
My hands and my feet
But so glad was I, to see it destroy
Sand castles on its way up the beach
As the very uneven nature of sands
That is left behind (by the waves)
On it's way back into the sea
Reminds me of nothing more than
A sand wave of artificial developments
Faked out of a background
That is in itself nature

Many are moved by the power of nature
And most will forever and always be
But I remain unmoved and untouched
Yet happy, elated and most sensitive
For I have seen and realized that
The pretty blue sea could be as friendly

let me be your absent friend

And as bland as its hands
Yet remain a blue sea and no great reformer
I am no more a Child I have grown up
And still unable to feel nor tell whether
The pretty blue sea has grown up or not
But the last time I was by the beach
The pretty blue sea smelled like a friend
It presented me with fresh winds
And even some pebbles to throw back
So I could watch the smooth faced pebble
As it hits its face like the devil's
But I knew that, upon whatever face,
The pretty blue sea deem fit to present
The pebble will bounce but not hurt,
Before sinking or being swallowed by the sea
Like all family of stones

So why am I feeding the sea
If the same pretty blue sea
That was as friendly
As the best of life can be
Could be more threatening
Than a friend's care

Miami Beach, Florida. USA (September 2002)

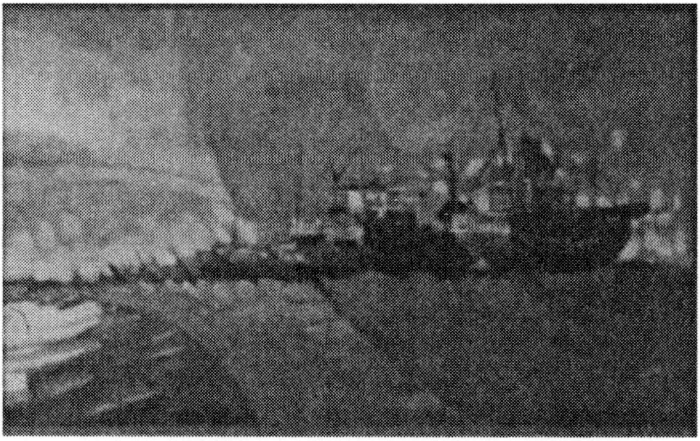

let me be your absent friend

Catacombs

Your smile said it all
That you were not flashing your teeth
Because of the blazing sun
And neither was your squinted posture
Adopted for the sake of exacting a measurement
-Under a Pharaoh's nest
Never the less it was most assuring to hear… when
You said you were hale and hearty
And your Wholeness of self is as clean
As a recently probed chimney
Yet you remained camped by a Catacomb!
Why for God's sake why!
When it has always been clear to all that
The family of Catacombs, like all bolted abodes
Are popularly known for the germs
They carry in them rather than the remains
Of its only occupants.
Their pains, their sorrows and even denials
Surrounding their death - we've all
But listen to…

Moody Beach, Wells, Maine. USA (July 2003)

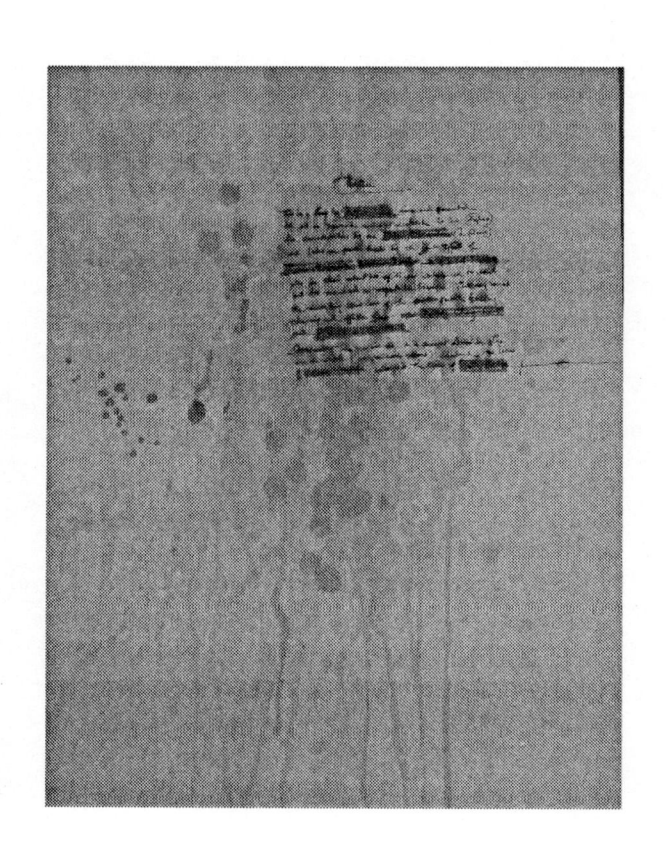

let me be your absent friend

Miss H P Bills

Her Father had high hopes for her
And so was her sweet singing Mum...
Ever glad to be with a wishful husband
As the little wet-eyed beauty, Hope
Was their only Daughter

And they could only hope for a life
Better than the one they themselves knew
"Someday in the nearest future
A worthy fella will come to tender
The petals of our pretty Hope"

Days, Nights and in between Seasons
They held fast to their hopes for Hope
Wishing her the best of all choices
Whilst they in turn put in their best
For Fame and Fortuna to smile their way

All for the love of their wet-eyed beauty, Hope.

Her shoes - right from her tender age
Were carefully selected. Not for their colors
But more for their classic English wideness of form
For a growing Lady like pretty Hope
Should not grow up sporting silly thumbs

They thought her to sit
As the art of abusing the surface of a chair
Elegantly, with her weight is another telling act

That separates the field of Ladyship
From the pedestrian path of a Mistress

Listening and talking comes to Hope, naturally
As she grew up to note as told
But not copy her parent's idiosyncratic style
For she was supposed to, and must always remain
Pastel groomed forever and always

And this was part of a recipe for Hope and a good life.

Her character at the age of twelve
Had been perfectly groomed but not well shaped
For what the demands of her time might be
So pretty Hope looks at life from a glass
Dried, drained and made to fit her family's need

By fifteen, she was the most popular at school
And peers of no noble standards (so they all think)
Feel less privileged to ruffle feathers with her
Talk less of comparing notes of any social values
With pretty Hope Ekaterina Billinsgate

Soon she took to signing her name as H P Bills
With what she thought was the most perfect style –
Grand, classical looking, well inclined and interactive
Handwriting, a most suited and revealing custom
for a Lady
She was made to believe by her parents at home

For all that was expected of her will soon be.

let me be your absent friend

Sometimes she loves to be as casual as one of the girls
But the idea of being one of the girls, for real!
Her Mum and Dad finds too irksome and repulsing
For being seen, stringed together
With the reckless temperament of Subalterns

Is incompatible with her pre-eminent grooming.

So pretty Hope in her teens
Was left with grand and mostly elevating choices.
This is her parents dream - coming into view -
As a resigned commission away from their class
Into one that is well suited for wealth

Before power and influence.
And now, in full view, lies some of those choices
That she's never been brought up to make - imagine
Pretty young Hope, turned and shaped as a social climber
And even molded like a Politician -

Aspiring for the most glittering living standard of all
The only consent she's got to give is her past
As some conscious fella's Daughter below the stairs
But can our pretty Hope dance and swim through
Her life's living commission?

As decisions all along have always been her parents.

Well, this is what we are about to see
True reality and the effect of a transformation
As opposed to one synonymous with change
On the life of a living descendant of mother Eve
Hope Ekaterina Billinsgate a healthy looking baby girl

As certified at birth in the registry office
None could have predicted on her first breath of life
That little Hope –
a girl born into a Rat Catcher's family
Would ever be blessed with any degree of popularity
That if lucky would spread beyond

The threshold of her father's door, talk less of his farm
But her teachers in school knew better than most
They refused to be outstripped by a student's parent
Determination and diligence for their pretty Hope
To be Elegant, polished and better than most

Superficially,

So they tried their best to make hers a mind capable,
Well grounded, charming, amiable and as clever as she could handle
Rather than pressed for outstanding brilliance and consistency
Like her parents, they tried their best in all ways, but failed
To feed her mind about her future on a path so filled

With clever ways and pretentious intents of good-natured boys
So, poor Miss H P Bills, in her desperate attempt
To quickly loose her baggage like all teenage years
Was ingloriously felled in her tracks
By the sharp edge of a tongue and not a sword

As religious fencing was an art she's never begged for…
Though determined and focused to drink from a good well
As Mum and Dad had always wished for
She won the trust of many wealthier acquaintances
And topped the list of their glittering parties

And many endless social occasions

Where most boys would rather win her as a priced governess
In other to gain an amount of a handsome curiosity -
The type that only a Rat catcher's offspring could offer
Before loosing the favor, the pity and the challenge
That only aging could offer

After all she aimed to be one of us, was their watchword
But pretty Miss H P Bills held her ground and her dignity
Until one fateful evening, when like an insulting epigram
The valued wit of Miss H P Bills and her craftiness
Was measured and selfishly outclassed by another upstart

Soon she was out on the road, cruising along in a big car
And dancing to the tune of another rat and a quiet pretender -
Decked in the robes of a charming Prince
He was everything in the world
That Mum and Dad had never prepared her for

But pretty Hope in her mind, would settle for nothing more…

For the moon shall nest tonight (if possible) by her will.
And the charming Prince, another upstart in his calculative way
Remained camouflaged from her gentle camp. To him
He has just won himself the most deserving of all fishes
And to her – this is the fulfillment of a life's passion

Mapped out for so long and due to be harvested
By one she considered most qualified. For the breath
Of a Billinsgate on a public face, shall no longer be
(From today and other days to come) the only one
That is mostly given to the charitable convention of all

So here we are
In the party of two selective and highly discriminating minds
Sitting and cruising along by each other side
And comfortable so far and so to say in each others shadow
With each other's mind playing each other's game

He faked many stories for her ears to listen to and to take to heart

When in actual fact, his decision to do so
Remains unknown to her. So too were her gestures
Her bland but highly consuming expressions
Were well rehearsed, perfected and well practiced to fool
Enough to deceive and to cajole without intimidating

let me be your absent friend

As there remains a prize for being mysterious.

Yes, there is always a prize lurking behind closed doors,
And there will always be a set of eyes waiting
To explore whatever might be in those shadowy corners
But whatever it may be, in this camping party
Is obviously governed by a different kind of truth –

And rather than seeing the true truth itself, at play,
An ideal refugee has been employed in its place
As both parties are bent on a desired quest to impose
A commitment of forcing a dream on each other
But before we could become parties to their errors

Or even become highly consumed in the flame of their ways
The blaring sounds and the illuminating lights of an officer
Suddenly unmasked the colorful journey of H P 's Prince
As a life that is better heard of than been lived.
Another life overloaded with the highest degree of needs

Suddenly, all that has been carefully hidden by the Prince

Was out in the open for the world to see. And an Unlucky Miss H P Bills (a victim) with her well groomed manners

Ended up in jail on her first real date. Her crime -
Getting caught cruising but not canoodling in a stolen car
Two minutes before her twenty first birthday -

One, which she celebrated in a cold Banger
And there, alone, in a cold cell, sits the Rat Catchers pride
At a time when she never wished for the world's eye
On her presence, there, she was, sitting, all by herself,
Waiting to be bailed from a life that seems so far away

From the reality she's always courted
Can she ever remain herself after this?
Or will she be too much a reality herself?
I cannot tell, for doing so will be against
My wishes. And I'd rather not impose

Nor debase your mind any more than this…

Moody Beach, Wells, Maine. USA (July 2003)

let me be your absent friend

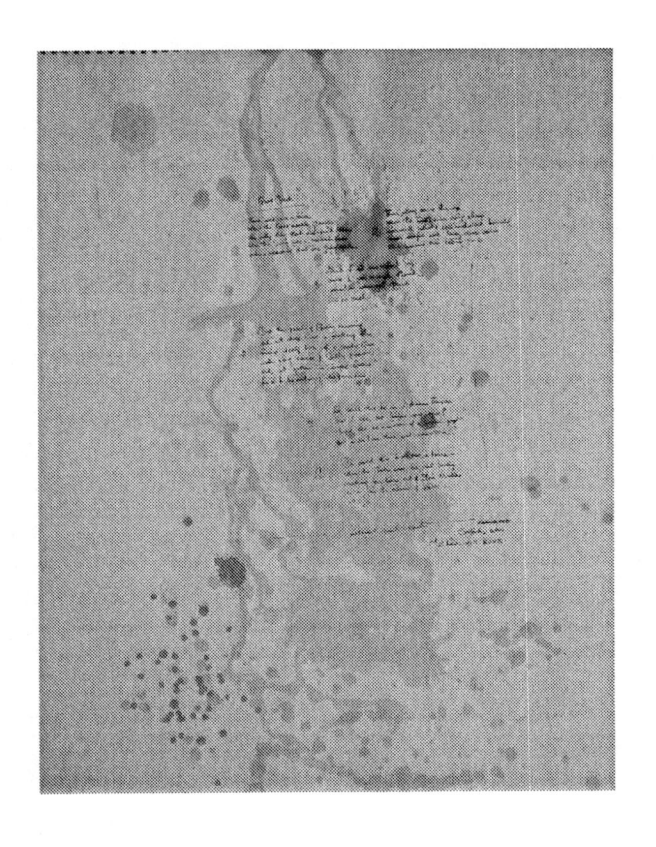

The problem of undressing a first love

Knowing that Moma was not there
To give her Son a helping hand
And Papa was nowhere to be found
To talk this loving player through –
At a time when required most,
I remember my fear and my anxiety
As the mixed emotions, I experienced
When faced with the problem
Of undressing my first Love

At the beginning, mounds upon mounds
Of strange things kept popping out at me,
All right from behind the blouse
And surprisingly, they all have a life
Living in them.
Stopping at this stage, I guess will be seen
As been stupid and fumbling through
As I have been doing looks very silly
But with the way things are going,
I think I'd prefer to pay a price for both –
Being silly and stupid all together.

Wish I had the patience to examine
The moving ground upon which I stood,
And maybe doubt my own vision or
My ability to reason before becoming
Too occupied with this embrace of the belly.
But its grip on the body is quite different
From those ever presented to me by
Those glossy pictures on glossy pages.

Damn it, you give so much
To those pictures and they in return
Never stop jumping at you

But then, that's all you could ever hope
To get from those naked pictures,
Unless you are into the art of sticking pages
Together, like most Guys do.
Now I know better as I have just fumbled
My way through this benefit, I mean
The benefit of engaging in a locking game,
The type that leaves players
Empty in daylight, pig headed at night
And at times, most players come out
As if they have just been strangely blessed
With an immeasurable pleasure…

Miami Beach, Florida. USA (May 2003)

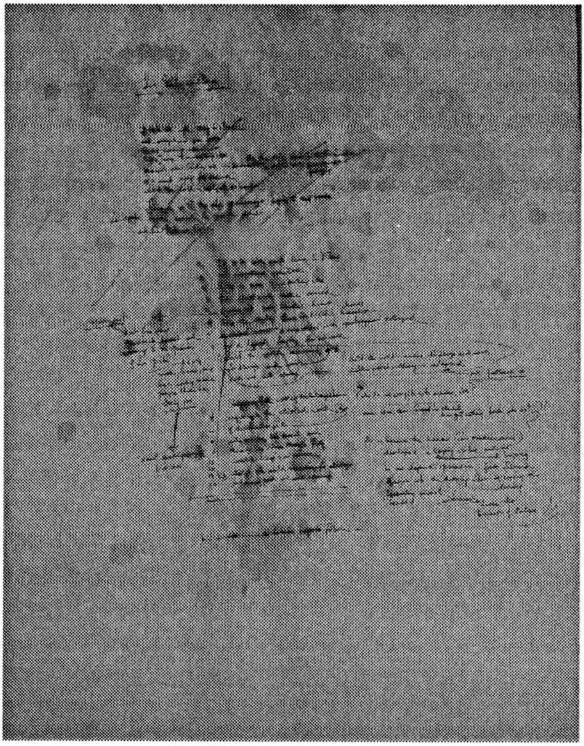

let me be your absent friend

To Nina Korman

If there are other ways
Of saying thank you
Or of showing gratitude,
Then,
I would have said it
And even displayed it,
Before returning it to you -
Without writing a single line,

But, since I cannot match
A penny for a pound and
Neither could I afford to
Trade a nickel for a gold…
I must say that your contribution
Made very special,
A rather unusual night –
When amidst strange faces,
I, with my affected skill,
Spend my art on others heart.

And with your assistance,
I, like a skillful Captain,
A Skipper, a daring Pilot,
But not a grand enough for
The stuff that Knights
Are known to be of,
Was able to set the night
On a grand and extremely
Delightful course.

So, thank you Nina,
Thank you, Ms Korman.

Miami Beach, Florida. USA (March 2002)

Dear Sgt Major

With so reluctant a heart
And a mind so groomed
On not letting my mates down,
I wish I could have done better
Than to resort to this,
But since time, surprise and
Unforeseen circumstances
Provided me with less than
Required, I guess I could
Only resort to the fact that
I will be denying myself
The ample opportunity
Of being able to practice
My trade at the war front
My reason for this is that
I accidentally mowed my toe
Whilst tending the Missus garden
The night before the previous
And I am very sad to say that
I'll miss the war in Iraq
As ordered by the President

Tell my colleagues in arms
That because of this accident,
I will not be there
To happily share or partake
In sharing the pain and the glory
Of a war front in Iraq
And neither will I be there
To happily parade and partake
In sharing the glory

Of a heroes welcome
After the war in Iraq

For me, medals of valor
Will be missing from my chest
This time around
And for many seasons,
The best plays from this war
Will forever be missing
From the lips of someone
Who knew about the flavors
And the spices contained
In those bright stories
That all heroes are known to tell

But with the blessing
Of my young Missus,
I promise to do my best
By constantly supporting them
-The troops, from home
All through this war

And If after this war
I ever make it through the ranks,
I promise, I will induct
The young ones, my mates,
My troops, all of their mates
In other troops and hopefully
The combined forces in general,
To please desist from last minute
Gardening and other activities
That their calculative Missus
Might throw their way

let me be your absent friend

Just before leaving home
For future engagements

Have a good war

Your most loyal trooper
Jack "Irish Goodwar" Sillitoe

Miami Beach, Florida. USA (March 2003)

I played my bit

I played my bit
Whilst my teeth
Were busy rattling

Yet I was so lucky
They did not fall out
Nor even chip a bit

Now I could wait
To watch the Sun set
From Chelsea piers

And Folks could see
How white my teeth
Had suddenly become

When summer comes

Chelsea, New York. USA (January 2003)

let me be your absent friend

Shuffling towards senility 1994 London
Charcoal on paper
Abosede Gladness

Dance, as an art that we engage in, is another step towards a certain type of reality in human life. The beginning of which requires a degree of reasoning and excitement for no sane person will dance in order to disgrace him or herself...

"my body is no longer a church but a living exhalation" - (Olive Sewell-Smith, 2000)

167

The angry Air

An angry air, whose refreshing qualities
Were once like a freshly laundered sheet,
Decides that time is ripe
To display its measure of power
It welcomed a friend – a Vagabond
And fellow ruffler, who upon request
Launched its best known characteristics
-Anger, through architectural openings
It tore apart curtains and blinds
And all other objects that were meant to
Curtail its ever-robust entrance
By gently swaying and shaping its direction

But the exuberant air loves its power,
It therefore made the frail fabric yarn, shiver
And the soldiers of plane white blinds, rattled
As the unseen (to human) but highly felt
Hands of the all-cleansing wind
Manage to ease the labored anguish
Of having to wash away
Musky moistures that humans do crave for,
For conditioning different skin types

And most could vividly recall
How the musky moistures
Dried up whilst they remain seated,
Feeling drunk from a conditional pleasure
As the soothing hands of the wind
Continued lapping up gleaming moistures
And other bodily wastes

let me be your absent friend

In the end,
The cynical air and its friends thus asked
If we as humans, could have been more favored,
To retain the fragrance of our sweats
If scrubbed clean with fresh water and no air...

Manhattan, New York. USA January (2003)

New York

Over there, in New York,
Beauty is clothed, but not dressed
As nobody's got time to spare
Neither was a dime ever spared

There is neither a night
Nor will there ever be a day
As colors and tones of beauty
Remain for ever disjointed
Like another garment

Architectural facades and life
And everything in New York
Hangs – not in full garment,
But in individual patches

Manhattan, New York. USA (January 2003)

let me be your absent friend

The last Star shines the most

Having lost others, Peers,
Without whom a familial trace
Would never have being -
The brave widowed form,
Of the last Star,
Still shines the most.

Having lost others, Peers,
With whom you once shared
The same role in space -
The brave widowed form,
Of this last Star,
Still shines the most.

Yes,
They were, and might have been
Your equal, in fate but not in fame
And will most likely remain so…
… In the eyes of all concerned,

But for whatever it is…

I, somehow, envy the last Star
For what might have being
And not for that, that will soon be,
As I do not wish, for the
Tyranny of its loneliness

'specially now,
That it pretends, to shine, the most

Miami Beach, Florida. USA (April 2002)

let me be your absent friend

The joy of Castle Rising

In those days of Norman England,
The widow of King Henry I, used to
Welcome well wishers to her Castle
With a drink of Castle Rising,
Before giving them a tour of her
Magnificent Castle; that was built
Of Barnak stone in the year 1138 AD.

But the North being so plain and windy,
Was always ready to blow the headgear
Off the head of Her Majesty's visitors

And Her Majesty being an embodiment
Of taste and style, refused to believe that,
It was a case of one drink too many.

So Her Majesty made a resolution –
"For all that Norfolk breeds, be ye
Warriors, workers and builders alike,
Support your heads with your hands
And enjoy the view of Castle Rising".

But Northern Folks being so plain and
Humble, were always ready to merry
And cheer to their Royals delight,

And that was when they all realized
That, it was no longer a case of one drink
Too many.

So Her Majesty devised another noble

Style "for all that passes through Her
Land and all that lives on the vales and
Humps of suburban Norfolk, before you
Can see the beauty of Carstone made, use
A ligne de tete to hold your hats in place,
And you will see the joy of Castle Rising"

Buckingham, England. UK (January 1998)

let me be your absent friend

A seduction of Innocent throats

With a feast of grapes from the Alps
And the magic of slow fermentation,
I hereby seduce all Innocent Throats!
Enjoy the sensuality of late maturation
And the slight hint of wonderful aperitif,
Not harsh but fruity, clean and delicate,

Harmonious than Bacchus ever provided.

I command ye golden birds and diamond geezers
Purify your hearts! You double minded gits,
Commit yourself to a definite persuasion,
For the rewards of many, but one hangover
Is always better than missing a good length
Of exotic Swiss wines, on your palates.

I pity advances, when rejected
And friendly gestures, when ignored
But I, will continue in my honored quest
And my commitment, to always seduce
Innocent throats
And my attempts will not be fruitless,

For Innocent Throats does not despise…

Buckingham, England. UK (February 1998)

A bottled condemnation

Although we feel them, rather than learning about them;
Those red and urine colored, intoxicating liquids,
Do tend to be blessed with tasty tentacles, especially,
When they do besiege thy lips and trickle down
Thy throats, like fluttering sea waves.

Those who feel it, swallow, while enthusiasts' gaggle,
But blessed is he who sings its most enchanting praises,
Of passions, derived from trickling pleasurable desires
Like Lorenzo da Ponte's 'ditirambo sopra gli odori'
A post renaissance song, dedicated to the glory of wine

For passions are derived from pleasurable desires.

Human desires do have its upper, over reasoning
And maybe happy endings do have its own meaning
But, whenever Grapes are ripe enough to be picked,
The patient wine farmer is always very pleased
To make the grapes pay their debts: for being fit

For harvest and for a bottled condemnation

Buckingham, England. UK (March 1998)

let me be your absent friend

Between hanging and mid life crises
"between hanging and mid life crises, I prefer death"...
he said to the Judge

He was somebody's Son, Brother
And maybe Uncle to some Other,
Yet nobody showed up, for him.
None from his own kin showed up
To bid him well on his last trip
Never the less
He made his way to the gallows.
He stepped forward, with an ivory
Look on his face
For he knows what will become of him
In the final hour of his last breath

He knew his body would jerk violently,
His spinal chord will plastically stretch,
He knew his neck would snap
And be held aloft at an angle,
Yet he was happy that his last gift
For the cleaning world will not be blood…

But a streak of very hot shit
Splattering down his legs
Whilst departing this world
With bulging eyeballs

Whilst others with their mid life crises
will enviously say
"At least he knows what's to become of him"
Rather than spend a lifetime pondering
About a life that might not open a path for him,

He went through it his way – the best he could
And as he understands it most

Violence was the only power he knew
Even as he walked to his death
Knowing he was going to arrive
At a heaven's gate – a disabled man

Yet his last breath was publicly paid for
Whilst most in their mid life crises
Will forever remain outraged
By the nature of their own passion -
The anger they could not afford to love.

Miami Beach, Florida. USA (September 2002)

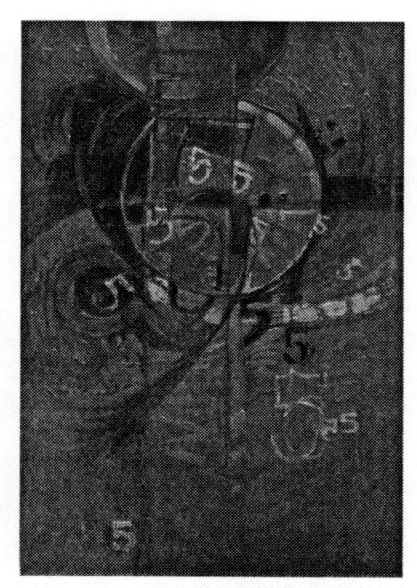

let me be your absent friend

La pieta en Roma

In Rome, I saw a mother
Busy lamenting the death
Of her grown up Son,
As if He is still an Infant
Lying across Her arms

Her pity was encased in marble
And her dream – though humble,
Was far from Herod's wish
One she defeated in His infantile

But her dreams once captured
In marble, remains fresh
And her pity forever young

So my dearest friends,
If it is ever cold in Rome
And you are not far
From St Peter's,
Snuggle up to the fabric
Of La Pieta

And the amount of heat
Gathered and enshrined
By Michelangelo's hand
Will, I hope,
Keep you warm

VSC Johnson, Vermont. USA (June 2002)

To my Grandmother (the illiterate)

Your silent voice I follow still, Grandma,
Your silent voice I follow still.
Even now, as I try to steady the muse
From tumbling-off from my lips
Your silent voice, I follow still
And even now that my teenage charge
Seems to probe your literariness,
Your silent voice, I follow still.

Your wise words, I gambled away
Thinking they were the chilling words
Of an illiterate, as I was too engrossed
In myself, to place any value on them,
Yet, you, Grandma, with your kindness,
You never for once laughed out
At how anyone like myself
Could remain so clowned in my own
Childish gown

When I thought I was the informed one

Never did it occur to me that my literary self
Would never have been at all
Without the playground of your satires,
Your metaphors, your allegories
Your mythologies and those other stories
That you Grandma, use to tell me

Now I feel like a prodigal Son
Your prodigal Son, Grandma

let me be your absent friend

I have spent all your endorsements
Along with the contents of your charities
I have spent your only gift to this world
Without thinking about their origins,
From your songs to your arts and
From your styles to your literatures –
All because I think I was a literary being

But despite my reckless regard, Grandma
My garden of youth you still tender
As you've always done
With your loving care, you shaped,
Nurtured, structured and tuned me
Like a guitar
All because you want your Grandson
(A prodigal one for that matter)
To stay and to remain in tune

Whilst I was busy pretending to be a literary being

But since your democratic patience means
I could still be heard in the court of your heart,
I believe, it is better to seize this moment
To apologize, in favor of my arrogance

That:
I am not guilty of spending your oral stories, Grandma,
Because I do not want to give praise to your allegories
For the plain inductive nature of your satires
Are like the Old World …always designed to control
By whatever means

That:

I am not guilty of spending your metaphors, Grandma,
Because of my wish to live a life devoid of stories
For the plain inductive nature of your stories
Are like the Old World... always designed to control
By whatever means

That:
Maybe I was guilty for not giving praise to the illiterate
Because living this life, I see as my greatest choice
And the tyranny of spending all that is yours, Grandma,
I see as my preference... for this is a New World
By every means

VSC Johnson, Vermont. USA (June 2002)

let me be your absent friend

The young Girl and the Tree

The young Girl said to the Tree "I play with you,
I don't know why, but I will remain nice to you,
Since you, with your many shades, sheltered me
Many times, from the burning Sun"

Her youthful world, now, begins to crumble
And Her life, slowly began
To pave way for the dawn of adulthood,
Her heart – another world, She's never noticed,
Slowly, begins to evolve within Her

This - a transformation She never knew existed
Nor even noticed, within Her own self
As Her mind, was now becoming like a Cloud,
Constantly moving and as always, pre-occupied.

But given Her price, for being Human,
Who knows, She might have tried to exert a control
And stop nature dead on its track, thus
Deny Herself (a fresh and promising little Bird)
The joys of leaving Her marks on Innocent Trees

Deny herself
The joy of forsaking the devil in the Other life,
From a certainty, that She will soon grow
to become a Lady
And like all Ladies,
would take to carving out Her name
On the bark of Innocent Trees,

And the trees in return,
Will soon grow accustomed to rousing her
To the core, filling Her with rapture
And making sure Her shoulders, like all shoulders,
Shuddered, and squeezed, like ripe Oranges,

Then followed
With Her smile… constantly complimented
Like flowers are, under the blanket of a yellow Sun

Miami Beach, Florida. USA (September 2002)

The garden of my youth

Still lives and long shadows, lolling
Amongst silver dews and golden leaves,
All marking an ascent – My ascent
Into manhood – My manhood

In the garden of My youth
There were many trees,
So many…and all, taking roots
And all helping themselves

Or rather myself – in My prime,
To shape My form and also theirs,
In the mold of what I am today
And what I am likely to become

By night or evenfall.
But since drawing symbols and parallels
In between this important stage
Had been mine and is still mine,

Then I suppose, that I, myself
As the only leaf amongst green grasses,
Could very well defy their roots
And allow myself to grow wild -

As the call of nature so determines,
Since the long shadows and its shades
Do not really occlude and
Since I could see through the nature

Of silver dews in it's true form

Or even enrich the pear shaped dewies
With the physical quality of a golden leaf...
And that, I see fit, as I am, now

Miami Beach, Florida. USA (March 2002)

Strange things and Common places

Had it not been for your intent – as revealed,
I find my inner noise more trusting, and would have
Continued quietly, with my quest about vulgar traits
And official Architectural statements
But as my mind was busy shaving the dusts
Off the face of a portico that was really struggling
With the lingo of choice, used for the volumnal mass
Around it, talk less of the remaining façade,
That it has been made to be part of…

Before proceeding to inspect the loud tension
Resonating from the core of the building;
Wherefore, I notice the Clerk and a few Others
Sitting under a lavishly furnished dome - one
That was too provincially American and Modern,
Than being taken for a serious Roman or Classical.
Nevertheless, I concluded that it showed
Ingenuity and a highly superficial boldness…

But as my sweet memory was busy computing all
That I have just seen, as new, more than of feeling,
Nor of true understanding of how to use the old
And its affections, for evolving, rather than
Developing the new out of a Mickey's ghost…
I noticed you, and the cheeky anxiety in your posture,
As you walked in,

But why pretend to be a trusting spirit,
When a Civic pride has been so abused?
Why pretend to rouse feelings long dead,

let me be your absent friend

Betrayed, abused and so denied of its own tears
That, even, the Clerk – a Man, not a Woman
And certainly not a flower,
Suddenly grew sick and almost withered,
Like autumn leaves falling off mother trees,

But then,
The only thing the Clerk was capable of dropping
Whilst you hover and twirl around his desk,
Was the ball pen in hand, before his jaw
As you requested to be guided through
A procedure on how best to sue yourself,
Or to make a case for an un-civil behavior in Public
Your behavior of course

As you, a poor Artist and the most serious Clown
Ever, to tread the face of this Earth
Has just successfully passed wind
In front of the President
This year, 2003

Philadelphia, Pennsylvania USA (February 2003)

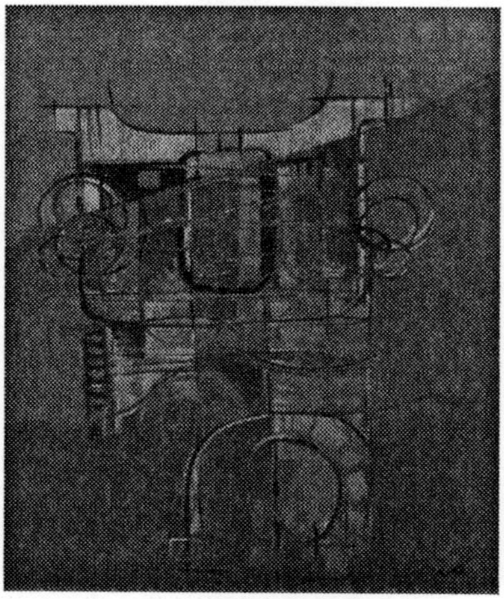

let me be your absent friend

Mrs. Jane Appletree

In those days, not too long ago,
When carriages were Horse drawn
On rusty tracks or cobblestones,
If lucky to be in the right part of town;
Or in those places where houses
And sidewalks were all
But lamp lighted with oils
Gotten from the belly
Of slaughtered Sharks…

I can guarantee, without doubt
That she would have been persecuted!
Yes, send to the gallows
Or made a brown bread
Like Joan of the Arc
As the bonfire lovers did
But this is a new millennium
And this is America (a new world)
And everyone could do as pleased

And so was our pretty young Lady,
Miss J, now Mrs. Jane Appletree.
Her Mother thought nothing
Of her actions, saying "at least
A Heritage and a Hussie, bound
Together in one's care,
And made accessible to the world's care,
Was certainly well thought off"
And her Father thought of her
Daughter, as being very smart indeed

For acting to protect her inheritance
In the most pre-emptive way

Her wedding made the headlines
And Jane was made popular, in fact
Popular enough to quietly disturb
And awaken all living Souls.
For hers reduced the Stars, the Bandits
The Politician and the Celebrities
To small-time Amateurs -
Too busy singing whilst trying to
Escape their own Guards.

So crazy Jane, pulled the fastest one
On a very sane World
She married one of the Trees
In her front garden
And kept her Boyfriend of five years
Still incubating in the house
She left all concerned, guessing
On who had ever been closer to Jane?
The nameless BF or Mr. Appletree

Now,
Mr. Appletree is more than an equal
In fate and in fame, to the Boyfriend
And he, the BF, with drooping shoulders
Like those of a grateful Dog
Could only wait for a Divine Favor
As any possible transgression or even
A gentle trim of Mr. Appletree's reach
Will arouse the flaming passion
Of many environmental Janeses

let me be your absent friend

Talk less of Mrs. Appletree, herself,
Her capital gains, her tax exemptions
And her friends from the Green Peace

Moody Beach, Wells, Maine. USA (July 2003)

A bad Shepherd, I wish to remain

A bad Shepherd, I wish to remain
For my precious energy, I will not waste
Chasing after a stray sheep
When there is always more to be gained
From my pride as a bad shepherd

The lost Dog or the stray Cat,
I will not chase, for a lost energy,
If lucky, can be regained
But an ounce of a depleted energy
Makes formidable, a failure, called luck
As it requires more than luck itself
To furnish, or to replenish

Therefore,
My precious energy, I will not waste
Chasing after a stray sheep
For there is always more to be gained
From the pride of being a bad shepherd

The cardigan of a bad Keeper of care,
Suits, and fit my like, very well
And before I wear it to a hell –
That I knew never existed,
As far as I do care, now,

Then, I swear that my time,
I will never waste, lifting up any, in repose

let me be your absent friend

When this life and my life,
Demands more of me than I can keep
For myself, or for the remainder of a flock
And any flock for that matter
So why waste time over a lost Dog?

The spirit of the lost Dog itself
stands for that of an adventure,
An Athlete and maybe, a Hero,
a spirit that craves liberty
And one that obviously exists
beyond the controlled field,
Of the one that I, pretending to be its guide
Can ever provide

So why try to make a fallen hero
Of all poor beasts, when a lost Dog
Like all spirits of adventure will always find its way

Moody Beach, Wells, Maine. USA (July 2003)

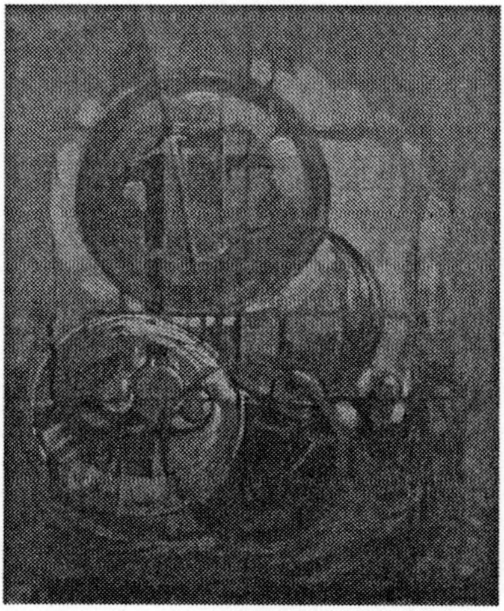

Kate Westcott

The journey was made easier.

Charcoal marks were beautified
Upon their contacts with plain paper
And the anonymity of poor plain papers
No longer prevails.

Grains and fibers becomes vulnerable
In the face of an assigned creativity
And your easel – like a helping hand,
Helped life off a burden
By making paper susceptible to pen

Now every mark is no longer a suspect
As charcoal sticks, glides through the surface
With poor plain papers unmasked
And marked for life
By the wily hands of the Artist.

Yet this experience, this journey
Of four weeks at VSC Johnson
Might not have been made easier
Without the gift of your easel
Thank you Kate, thank you,

For the paintings were as if yoked
By an invariable chord…

VSC Johnson, Vermont. USA (June 2002)

Certain things

Certain things do bear fruit
And certain things do hack fruit

The Chemist, with his variables, was here,
He tasted Art and his heart refused to go
And in comes the retired Surgeon,
The Physicist and also the Dentist –

All retiring to their fanciful hobbies –
Amateurs, painting landscapes in the park

They tasted Art and their hearts refused to go
Whilst the crafty Chemist mass produced
All organic, earthen and synthetic pigments

Ah… the business of art after all

And Art, once reserved lost its bearing

So beautiful Art, where art thou?
For our heart is no longer in Art
As your beneficiaries could no longer protect
A system that made your Art, an Art

The subject in your heart died of alienation
And the meaning of your Art died of loneliness,
Abandonment, death - as industrial decay
Now serves a varnish, sealing up your fate

let me be your absent friend

Whilst your beneficiaries could no longer protect
A system that took your Art to heart

VSC Johnson, Vermont. USA (June 2002)

History

History was
An Angel, yesterday,
Suddenly turned
A Saint, for today, and now
But fast becoming a Devil
For tomorrow

Moody Beach, Wells, Maine. USA (July 2003)

let me be your absent friend

The Body
My body is no longer a Church, but a living aesthetics

Armed with a degree of reasoning and
Excitement, I pretend to be sane, and
I tend my body, muscles, bones and all
As if atoning for a past – my own past
Whilst I keep myself fit for this present
And appropriate myself for future drawings
Yet this muscles and bones betray still…

A fragility born of elegance and piety
Yet this muscles and bones betray still…
A cloudy passion of grace and pessimism
Yet this muscles and bones betray still…

I walked, engaged and flattered all that is the body
And kept advancing towards a type of reality…
Yet my best kept going for cheap
Sentenced by this body, long before enacted

So I chose to dance in other to disgrace myself,
Onlookers called it comedy whilst their laughter
Another censorship, and a step away from tears
Enacted by same muscles and bones and all

That kept up its noble attachment…
A living edifice, which continued to betray still

Miami Beach, Florida. USA (February 2001)

Six feet under

Six feet under and still bearing grudges
That, those who shed tears
For you awhile ago,
And paid for diggers to dig you in,
Into your new house...
This depth – this sunless depth,
Where the Lord's Prayer has no merit,
Will soon be busy smiling,
Chatting, getting drunk, toasting
And if by chance, they happen to recall
Your absence – will not hesitate
Before clinking glasses to honor
Your absence

And you, can do nothing!.

You wish they had grieved
At the wrong grave, and
Rather than concentrate on your
Newly discovered silence
And the benefit of not being heard
Anymore...you still bear grudges
Forgotten that,
Soon, your fame will spread
Through the darkness of your space
Making descendants and heirs
Out of maggots – lucky fellas
who never cared for your grudges

Moody Beach, Wells, Maine. USA (July 2003)

La Citta del Sole

Take a look
At my house in the Sun
Its walls are cracking
And its lawn;
Dry and un-kept

Yet my heart
Keeps them together
My heart
Keeps them together

And with my breath
From afar
Its memory (I hope)
Will forever
Remain
Green

Miami Beach, Florida. USA (April 2001)

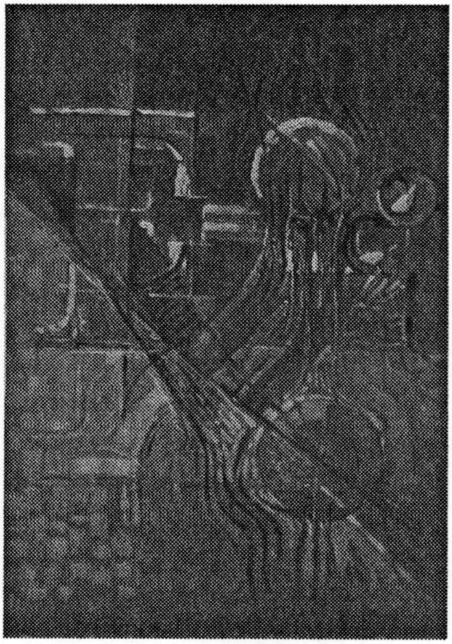

let me be your absent friend

The Green field

With a back to the ground
And a head held aloft;
On a summer evening,
I lay in a field,
Between tall grasses…
I am away from the woods
But not so far away,
From my family home
In Maine
The field becomes a place
Where blades of tall grasses
Behave like friendly winds
Hugging my head to the right -
If I turn that way
And also to the left,
If I choose to go that way
As the green field tells me
Of many more green grasses
To hug like a friend
As the night goes by
And also
As I count the stars in the sky
I also follow the moon
On many other nights
When there are no stars
Moving around in the sky
For me to see
With my back to the ground
On a green field
In Maine, New England

Just behind my family home
At night

Time to go now
Goodbye

Moody Beach, Wells, Maine. USA (July 2003)

Tree talk

1st tree talks:
To say that I have been defined
By others' correspondence is almost true
But for how long will I remain
A tree, an organic element, another part of nature,
A fair characterization and a romantic alternative

2nd tree laments:
If I had been named a Rose
My name would have been encased in beauty
I would have been food for many thoughts,
A symbolic dress for many desires
And all the pleasures that many do humanly seek

3rd tree comments:
There is more to see in the sky
Than there were – dark Roses
For humanity in its happiest state
Needs no flower to confess a love

1st tree talks again:
Appearance, habitations and projections
Have strengthened my speech – as an organic specie
And the changes of many a lifecycle means
I do not belong here or there anymore

2nd tree chips in:
You do not belong here or there anymore!

I suppose if being in others eyes does not always mean
Being – in there comprehension

Then the dignity of being anonymous in my domain
I no longer enjoy

3rd tree comments again:
There is no need to enjoy anything
When the benefits of real transformation
Will always remain a dream –
Somebody's utopia, lost in organic projections

1st tree reflects
Fresh, young and tender was I
A plant, glittering like a golden corn,
I bore no protective armor, when
I was raised from the ground

2nd tree agitates
I am a nature's knight, without a sword
I am given to giving without rewards
I am friend to Friends and Foes alike
I deserve more than this…

Miami Beach, Florida. USA (November 2000)

let me be your absent friend

The treatment of Nature

The lone bench sitting in the park
Once, was part of a whole
Still is and will always remain
That thing with a mind of its own
And maybe the only thing
That refused to stand up
Like everything else in the park

Gracefully it is that as a bench,
Cheating by sitting alone in the park,
It lives its days out in the open
Wherefore the open abode
Under the sun and the cloudy sky
Beyond its reach – admirably
Remains its God given domain

Though its posture now, as a bench
Canoodling in the park, is mostly at ease
As it embraced more – those elements
That are closer to the ground than it was
In its previous life, atop and as part of a tree
Where a duel with birds and bees
Was far from being absence

But God gave us dominion over others
And this baby's hand, we tore off
Away from its mother's robe,
And the mother's trunk, we injured
In other to rearrange our cities,
Our malls and our parks,

Various forms of reasoning
And possessions, we have used
To pervert their natural world,
In other to suit ours – organic,
One that we taped and ruled
From the coffee tables of our minds

Stewardship, as God's gift to others
We resigned and condemned as a dream
That no two Persons will dare look
Nor border to reconvene, harmoniously
Making so poor our credentials
That most in favor of a lone bench
That refused to stand up in the park

Are eager to embrace a maddening frenzy
When the vogue of a Conqueror
Shall no longer be a ritual – ours
To celebrate
And all things of nature
Would then laugh the last

Miami Beach, Florida. USA (November 2000)

I paid a price under a tree

It is normal for silly little birds
To fowl the leaves on trees,
For they, like other creatures of nature,
Would rather be good to nature
Than be its prodigal

It is normal for crafty spiders
To display their constructive skills
On trees
For they, like other creatures of nature,
Recognize them as their habitat

They need not have a settled income,
Yet they feed day to day,
For true nature needs not exact a price
Upon the portion of space
That belongs to birds and spiders

They are in nature, and are part of nature
And even if fowling the face of nature
Is part of their public shows
Then it has never been perverted
Like those of us –

Humans, sinful servants of pleasure
Exacting before extracting a price
On any portion of ground
That you and I may stand or sit in
Under these trees

Miami Beach, Florida. USA (November 2000)

Patience is a Fool's gift

Wish I was blessed with the patience of a tree
But, I, being Human, need not be rooted,
So I was blessed with the patience of a Rose
One whose allegiance is transcendental…

Miami Beach, Florida. USA (November 2000)

A concert in the wind

I once witnessed a concert in the wind
With a congress of fresh enharmonic leaves
Providing a rustling and a steady rhythm.
I recall the image of an upright Conductor -
Fully decked in a mosaic of sand colored bark,
Flailing and wailing through its slender stalks,
Whilst reminding the dropping mangoes
To please provide a loving cadence
Before the tenor of their sweet golden flesh
Become another sweet blend –
That sweetly mellow
The working parts of an earthly beings jaw

Miami Beach, Florida. USA (November 2000)

Walk away with me

As I make my exit,
My shadow, I am sure
Will walk away with me
And the image, left
In my wake, shall be
Like my passion –
Stronger than death,
And fully blessed with
An unlimited hope
Which, in my life's
Execution, I shall
Nourish appropriately
When required most,
And watered carelessly,
If a hole is about to burn
Through the soles of my
Sunny sandals
I shall loosen the threads
At the edge of my cuffs,
Salute all listening ears
By presenting a charming lyric
In other to sweetly cajole
Before offering a threat
To everyone's fidelity and
The ways and manners
Of your concern
For the life of an artistic poet
Is not as true as the way of love
But this written piece
Is like the way of love

Its fullness is an imposition,
From a bemused duty –
One whose sweat should not be
Judged nor justified by the way
Its fruits have been planted
So read on my friends
As I hope I haven't
Endangered your hope

Miami Beach, Florida. USA (November 2000)

let me be your absent friend

Papertalks

Horrible reader! you are warned,
This object before you is a book
And I suppose it is meant to be read,
Because,
It could as well double as a door stopper.
But while I'm open before your
Ciggy-stained breath and twitching face,
I must warn you!!!, to read seriously
Before the ink, rubs off my face.
Do not scratch my face with pen or pencil,
Neither should you mark with felt pen,
Be it of a toxic substance or non-toxic.
If you do!!, I will haunt you!
Believe me.
I've been recycled many times,
The last was as a toilet acquaintance;
I did so much to aid man's hygiene
But what was my reward as an arse bandit?,
A face-full of shit in the Loo
Whenever a human bowel opens up.
Now I am back with dual elements
Like Aristotle, I wake peoples mind,
Especially if they are willing,
Otherwise, I adopt the Baboon tactics
Like Alexander the Great;
I enjoy banging peoples head.
So do as I say
And read carefully.

Printed in the United States
19965LVS00001B/55